WHY DOES COFFEE MAKE YOU POOP?

The Ultimate Collection of Curious Questions and Intriguing Answers

Andrew Thompson

Published by:
ULYSSES PRESS
PO Box 3440
Berkeley, CA 94703
www.ulyssespress.com

ISBN: 978-1-64604-557-0
Library of Congress Control Number: 2023938267

Printed in the United States by Versa Press
10 9 8 7 6 5 4 3 2 1

Acquisitions editor: Claire Sielaff
Managing editor: Claire Chun
Editor: Beret Olsen
Proofreader: Barbara Schultz
Front cover design and layout: what!design @ whatweb.com
Production: Yesenia Garcia-Lopez
Artwork credits: see page 250

To Tom Phillips

CONTENTS

🤔 Why Is the Sky Blue?

One of the most commonly seen sights is the blue sky, yet what's not widely known is what makes it blue.

The sun emits light that travels through space toward Earth. Because space is a vacuum (i.e., it has no atmosphere), the light remains largely undisturbed until it nears the Earth, whose atmosphere is made up of a mixture of gas molecules (mainly oxygen and nitrogen) and other materials. The closer you get to the Earth, the thicker the atmosphere.

Light from the sun appears white but is in fact a combination of colors, and the range of these colors that are visible to the human eye—from red to violet, by way of orange, yellow, green, blue and indigo—is shown when light is passed through a prism. These different colors have different wavelengths and energies, with violet having the shortest wavelength and highest energy and red having the longest wavelength and lowest energy.

As light hits the Earth's atmosphere, the different colors react in different ways. Some of them get absorbed by the gas molecules while others do not. Most of the longer-wavelength colors (such as red and orange) pass straight through the atmosphere and are unaffected, while many of the shorter-wavelength colors (such as violet and blue) get absorbed by the gas molecules because the wavelengths (i.e., the distance between the peaks of each wave) of these colors are similar in size to the diameter of an atom of oxygen. The gas molecules then radiate these colors and scatter them across the sky, causing the sky to appear blue.

The reason why we perceive the sky as blue and not violet is because our eyes are more sensitive to blue.

❓ Why Are Moths Attracted to Lights?

It's commonly known that moths are attracted to bright lightbulbs and often circle them, giving rise to the saying "like moths to a flame." There are a number of theories as to why moths engage in this often life-threatening practice.

The traditional hypothesis is that moths mistake the light source for the moon. Moths are thought to migrate long distances, and it is believed that they use the moon to navigate on their journeys, it being a relatively stationary reference point from which to gauge direction. They can travel in straight lines by maintaining a constant angle to the moon. When the moth mistakes an artificial light source for the moon, it continues to keep a constant angle to the light. However, because of its close proximity to the light, this results in it spiraling toward it in a confused state.

While it's accepted that moths do indeed use the moon to navigate, the problem with the idea that moths mistake lights for the moon is that they tend to fly directly to a light and then spiral around it, rather than spiraling toward it as soon as they spot it.

A second theory is that moths fly toward lights in an attempt to keep warm. However, this has been discredited because it turns out that moths are more attracted to ultraviolet lightbulbs than those emitting normal visible light, which are warmer. In fact, moths are more sensitive to certain wavelengths of light—for example, they are more attracted to the colors in white light than to yellow.

A third theory—and the most compelling—is that moths are initially attracted to a light source and will fly directly toward it, but then, once there, will try to avoid the light and seek darkness (perhaps because they're nocturnal creatures). As a result of a peculiarity in the moths' vision, they perceive that the darkest place in the sky is an area about one foot from the light source. As a safety mechanism, the moth seeks out this darkest place and remains there, causing it to circle the light frantically within the dark band.

 ## Why Do You Sometimes See a Pair of Sneakers Hanging over Power Lines?

It is a common sight in many cities around the world to see a pair of shoes, laces tied together, hanging over a power line. Known as shoe tossing, it usually involves sneakers and is most prevalent in urban areas and college neighborhoods. Despite its widespread nature, it has evoked much curiosity over the years, and there is no universal explanation for the practice. Here are a number of theories.

- **Drugs.** One of the prevailing theories is that the sneakers are used to pinpoint a drug-dealing zone. They act as a sign to alert prospective purchasers that drugs are available nearby, so if a person loiters near the hanging shoes, a drug dealer may approach.
- **Gang turf.** The hanging sneakers may also indicate that a certain gang is claiming the territory. This is related to the

drug theory; if the area is home to a gang, drugs are also likely to be available.

- **Celebration.** The sneakers can indicate an act of celebration, marking a rite of passage, like a graduation from school or college. They have even been known to mark someone losing their virginity, or to mark an upcoming marriage. The custom may have originated with members of the military, who are said to have thrown their boots over power lines when they completed their basic training.

- **Commemoration.** People sometimes throw the shoes to commemorate the life of someone who has died. Legend has it that when the person's spirit returns, it will be able to walk above the ground, closer to heaven. They are also sometimes thrown to signal that someone is leaving the neighborhood and moving on to better things.

- **Bullying.** Many people believe that it is simply a form of bullying, the bully stealing someone's shoes and throwing them to an irretrievable place. Others say it's done as a practical joke played on drunkards.

- **Protest.** The sneakers may be thrown as a mark of protest against the government or other authority if community members are unhappy with a law or decision.

- **Art.** Yet another theory is that the thrown sneakers represent art, or a manifestation of the human instinct to leave their mark on their surroundings.

It's likely that one or more of the above theories are correct, and the precise meaning of the hanging sneakers may vary with the individual location. But one thing is for sure, the urge in people to launch their sneakers at power lines, in the desire that they remain there for posterity, seems to be undeniable.

Can the Great Wall of China Be Seen from Space?

It's commonly said that the Great Wall of China is the only human structure that can be seen with the naked eye from space or the moon. This proposition has been perpetuated in many sources: it's a question in the board game Trivial Pursuit, it has been contained in schoolbooks across the world, and it was stated as being the case by Ed Harris in the 1998 movie *The Truman Show*. In addition, *Richard Halliburton's Second Book of Marvels* makes such a claim, despite the fact that this book was first published in 1938, before the launch of any satellites!

One school of thought is that the claim was made to convey the enormous scale of the wall and the vast achievement in building it. It is now accepted that the proposition is false, however.

Many large-scale manufactured objects, such as highways, airports, buildings, and ships, can be seen with the naked eye, as can the Great Wall itself, but only from a low Earth orbit (up to about 200 miles above sea level). The wall's width ranges from about five to ten meters, but, when dust storms hit it, it becomes more visible at this close range. However, no human structures at all are visible with the naked eye above an altitude of a few thousand miles, and certainly not from the moon, which is about 240,000 miles away and from which entire continents and oceans are barely visible without mechanical assistance. These facts have been confirmed by a number of astronauts who have answered the question beyond any doubt.

Why Do We Yawn and Why Is It Contagious?

It has traditionally been thought that yawning is an involuntary reflex that draws more oxygen into our bloodstream and removes a buildup of carbon dioxide. This theory was fueled by the notion that when people are bored or tired, their breathing slows, resulting in a lack of oxygen, which causes them to yawn. However, research based on exercise suggests that this theory is incorrect. In tests, it was discovered that people's yawning rates were not altered during exercise, despite an increase in the breathing rate and levels of oxygen in the bloodstream. In addition, athletes often yawn before big events, which is unlikely to be as a result of boredom or a reduced level of breathing. It has also been found that fetuses yawn in the womb, even though they don't breathe oxygen into their lungs until after birth.

It has been suggested that people yawn to stretch the lungs, jaw, and facial muscles, which increases the heart rate and makes a person feel more awake, although this suggestion is largely posited on the fact that a stifled yawn that does not stretch the jaw is unsatisfying. Other theories are that yawning is used to regulate body temperature or is caused by a variation in certain chemicals, such as dopamine, in the brain. It is now accepted that the exact reasons why we yawn are unknown.

It's also not known why yawning is contagious. One theory is that we have evolved to yawn when others around us do because our early ancestors used yawning to coordinate social behavior or to build rapport in a group. When one person yawned to signal something, such as it being time to sleep, the rest of the group also yawned in agreement, and the members' activities were synchronized.

Yawning might also have been used to bare the teeth to intimidate enemies, so that, when one member of the group yawned, the rest followed suit. This has carried through to modern times, when the suggestive power of yawning is still contagious. Lending weight to this theory is the fact that babies, who are unaware of social codes, don't yawn contagiously until they're about one year old.

 ## Is One Dog Year Equal to Seven Human Years?

The age-old adage that one dog year equals seven human years derives from the simple mathematical division of the average human life span by the average canine life span.

It's true that dogs do age much faster than humans because of their higher metabolic rate; generally speaking, the larger the mammal, the slower the metabolism and the longer the life. However, it's now generally accepted that the seven-to-one rule

of thumb for a dog's "realistic" age is inaccurate; for instance, it's not uncommon for dogs to live to the age of fifteen, but very few humans live to 105.

It's believed that the seven-year rule should not be applied proportionally, and that, while it might be appropriate for the middle section of a dog's life, the beginning and final developmental phases cannot be correlated to those of a human. A dog tends to be fully grown and sexually mature at the age of one, but the same cannot be said of a human of seven. A more accurate method of calculating a dog's "realistic" age is to allocate twenty-one years for the first year (i.e., when dog and human both reach adulthood) and then four years for every additional year.

The size and breed of a dog are also factors that affect how fast it ages. Larger dogs age the fastest, so even the above rule cannot be applied to all breeds of dogs. In fact, the larger the dog, the more accurate the seven-to-one ratio becomes. Roughly, a large ten-year-old dog is considered to be seventy-eight, whereas a small ten-year-old dog would be fifty-six.

Why Is a Left–Handed Athlete Called a Southpaw?

The word "southpaw" is often associated with left-handed athletes, especially boxers and baseball pitchers. It is most commonly used in the United States.

Most sports pundits agree that Finley Peter Dunne, a journalist for the *Chicago News*, coined the term in 1885. The Chicago Cubs' home plate was oriented so that a right-handed batter (the most common type) would face east to avoid having the afternoon sun in his eyes. This meant that left-handed pitchers would throw from the south side of the diamond. These pitchers became known as southpaws.

Although it is generally thought that the term had its origin in baseball, the first recorded use of "southpaw" was actually in 1848, describing the punch of a left-handed boxer, who leads with the right and follows up with the more powerful left. This 1848 reference is long before the beginning of organized professional baseball and is quoted in the *Oxford English Dictionary*.

 ## Do Hair and Fingernails Continue to Grow after People Have Died?

The claim that hair and fingernails continue to grow for a period of time after a person dies is a myth. There is often the appearance that this has happened, but it is simply an optical illusion.

When death occurs, all of the cells in the body die, including those that generate hairs and nails, and the body immediately begins to dehydrate. This dehydration causes the skin around a person's hair and fingernails to retract, and it's this receding skin that gives the appearance that the hair and fingernails have grown, whereas in fact they remain the same length; it's the tissues in the skin that have shrunk. People expect hair and fingernails to grow, rather than skin to shrink, and this preconception can support the illusion.

The skin decomposes and shrinks at a faster rate than hair and fingernails, which remain intact for longer and so tend to stand out more prominently. This prominence also leads some people to believe that the hair and fingernails have grown postmortem. Funeral directors sometimes apply moisturizing cream to bodies as a measure to reduce skin shrinkage.

Why Do Quarterbacks Say "Hut!"?

The word "hut" is an interjection shouted by football quarterbacks to initiate a play. It doesn't mean anything in English, so how did it come about?

Monosyllabic words like hip, hup, and hep have been used for centuries to issue commands to animals. Herders used them for steering sheep, and carriage drivers called them out to direct their horses. They are short, sharp words that can be heard from a distance.

Drill sergeants in the early 20th century then started using similar words in rhythmic cadences for marching their troops. From the early 1920s, "hip, 2, 3, 4" was commonly used in this regard. By World War II, the sergeants began yelling "Atten-hut!" as a call to attention. The sharp sound of "hut" at the end of the word was used to make a platoon focus and listen.

In football, "hike" was the first of these types of words to be used. Prior to this, the quarterback would usually scratch the center's leg as a signal for the center to give the ball to the quarterback. But during the 1890–91 season, John Heisman (who later became a football coach and writer) was playing center for the University of Pennsylvania when an intentional leg scratch from an opposing player tricked him into hiking too early. To combat this scurrilous tactic, Heisman introduced the word "hike" to start the snap. The word already meant "to lift up" and had a short, sharp sound that worked well.

With the success of "hike," the similar sounding "hut" was introduced by the 1950s for the quarterback's cadence in calling the snap count: "Hut 1, hut 2, hut 3." Hut is short and sharp and can be heard clearly over a distance, making it perfect for football. Coming so soon after the war, it is almost certainly derived from the military drill sergeants.

Why Is New York City Called "The Big Apple"?

The origin of New York City's most famous nickname has been the subject of conjecture for many years. One view is that one New York guidebook to the houses of ill repute in the 19th century referred to New York as having the best "apples" (in this usage, a euphemism for prostitutes) in the world. Given that New York claimed to have the most and best brothels, it was inevitably called "the Big Apple." A second view is that the name was derived from a 1909 book by Edward S. Martin entitled *The Wayfarer in New York*, which made a reference to New York being the big apple and receiving more than its share of the "national sap." However, there is no evidence to suggest that either of these two sources had any influence on the popularity or spread of the term.

Many people believe that the name stems from a term used by jazz musicians to refer to New York, although it is thought that they did not begin the trend. That honor is believed to fall

to John Fitzgerald, a horse-racing journalist for the *New York Morning Telegraph*, who in 1921 wrote an article in which he referred to New York races around "the Big Apple." Fitzgerald claimed that he overheard the term being used by some African American stable hands in New Orleans, who referred to every jockey's dream being to race in New York because, "There's only one Big Apple. That's New York." The name was then popularized by jazz musicians in the 1930s because New York—and, in particular, Harlem—was the best place to perform and thought to be the jazz capital of the world.

In 1971, a New York advertising campaign adopted the name "The Big Apple" (using a logo featuring red apples) in an attempt to increase tourism to the city by portraying it as a bright and lively place rather than an urban netherworld rife with crime. Since then, the city has officially been known as the Big Apple throughout the world. In 1997, the corner of Fifty-fourth Street and Broadway, where John Fitzgerald lived for twenty-nine years, was named Big Apple Corner as a tribute to the man.

Why Are Mosquitoes More Attracted to Certain People?

Picture the scenario: You're at an outdoor barbecue, you decided to wear shorts, you don't have any insect repellent on, the sun has just set, and though nobody else seems affected, you're being eaten alive by mosquitoes. There is nothing more annoying! In between slapping your legs and clapping the air in frustration, you ponder, "Why am I being singled out?"

Around one in ten people are highly attractive to mosquitoes, and a lot of research has been done to find out why. Mosquitoes use smell to identify their prey, and they can detect human scents from up to 160 feet away.

Mosquitoes are particularly attracted to the carbon dioxide that we exhale. In addition to carbon dioxide, every time we exhale, we also release uric acid, octenol, and lactic acid. The specific combination of these chemicals in certain people makes them more attractive to mosquitoes. And it's not just the scent of this unique cocktail that mosquitoes are keen on; it's the quantity, too. Large people tend to exhale more, so they are prime targets, as are pregnant women, who exhale above-average amounts.

Besides this carbon dioxide concoction, mosquitoes like sweat, especially sweat that has combined with bacteria, also known as body odor. Everybody's odor is different and depends on the acids, ammonia, and other compounds emitted with the sweat. Mosquitoes prefer some mixtures to others. They also like heat, so a hot and sweaty person is perfect.

Blood type is the other key determinant of whether you'll be bitten more often. People with different blood types secrete different scents, and mosquitoes have been found to be twice as attracted to people with type O blood compared to those with type A blood, while those with type B blood fall somewhere in between.

And then there's this weird finding. A study found that significantly more mosquitoes landed on people after they had been drinking beer, although scientists could not fathom why. And it was only one study. One study isn't conclusive, is it?

In the end, our genetic makeup accounts for 85 percent of our susceptibility to mosquito bites, but to minimize your risk of being bitten, here's what to do: let everybody else do the running around, because their movement will attract mosquitoes, as will the excess carbon dioxide they expel by panting and the acids they exude by sweating. Your best bet is to lean back in a nice, comfortable chair and, after warning everybody else that beer attracts the little cretins, take the risk and drink it all yourself.

Why Does Touching Metal Sometimes Cause an Electrical Shock?

On a cold winter's day, you might experience an electrical shock upon touching a piece of metal. This type of shock is due to static electricity.

When two different insulating surfaces are touched together, opposite charges within the two surfaces are separated. Walking on a rug while wearing shoes is often enough to separate the negative from the positive charges, creating a surface charge imbalance on your shoes and in your body—the shoes pick up additional negative charges and leave positive ones behind, creating the imbalance. This rubbing of two nonconductive objects against each other generates static electricity, which you feel when you touch a metal object. This often occurs when a car door is opened.

Static electricity is more prevalent in environments with little humidity. This is why more electrical shocks are felt during winter, when humidity is lower. There are a number of items that, when rubbed together, typically create static electricity, but common ones are shoes rubbing against a floor and clothes rubbing against skin.

You can reduce the number of electrical shocks you receive. Increasing the humidity in the air is one way. Or ground yourself: touch the metal with something else first, such as car keys, which will receive the shock instead. Dry skin is also more susceptible to accumulating the electrical charges, so using moisturizer can minimize the shocks.

What Causes "Pins and Needles" in the Feet?

Commonly referred to as "pins and needles," paresthesia is the abnormal burning, prickling, or numbing sensation sometimes felt in the feet, legs, arms, or hands. It is not normally painful and usually lasts only a short while, with symptoms reducing once the affected limb is moved around. Some people say that the particular limb has "gone to sleep."

Paresthesia is generally caused by placing pressure on a nerve through lying on it awkwardly. This blocks the sensory messages sent to the brain, and the result is numbness. The tingling sensation occurs when the pressure is released and the nerves begin sending signals to the brain again. Pinched nerves that are compressed can have the same effect. Lying on a limb can also reduce the blood supply by compressing the arteries, and this can also produce "pins and needles." This is more common in the elderly, who sometimes have poor blood supply to the limbs because of hardened arteries or arthritis.

Certain medications, excessive alcohol intake, vitamin deficiencies, and diseases such as diabetes or multiple sclerosis can also cause the condition. Nerve damage can result in chronic cases of paresthesia, which can sometimes be relieved by physiotherapy or surgery.

🤔 Why Do Phone Numbers in Movies All Start with 555?

Phone numbers in movies and television shows usually begin with the fictional prefix 555. The reason why a fictional prefix was chosen for all on-screen phone calls is one of privacy.

A few decades ago, the first letters of exchange names were used as part of telephone numbers in the US, followed by numbers. The number five on the dial corresponded with the letters J, K, and L, but no exchange-name abbreviation could be made with any combination of these three letters. Instead, the 555 prefix was allocated to service providers' numbers, such as the directory assistance number, which is 555-1212. Anyone attempting to call a number used in a movie or television show would therefore be able to contact only a service provider, not a registered phone customer, which removed the potential for viewers to harass other customers. (There have been instances where 555 numbers were not used on television and a multitude of crank calls have been made to the number.)

In order to stop any further confusion from disrupting service providers, the numbers 555-0100 to 555-0199 are now specifically reserved for fictional use.

🤔 What Is the Origin of the Handshake?

Handshaking is a common method of greeting used across the world and is prevalent in both social and business settings.

Although most experts agree that handshaking is an ancient ritual, reported as far back as 2800 BCE in Egypt, there is some argument as to its exact origin.

Some say the handshake evolved from the practice of Egyptian kings shaking the hand of a deity's statue to transfer the god's power to the king. The Egyptian hieroglyph for the word "give" was an outstretched hand.

Most historians now, however, agree that the handshake's origin lies in fighting between men. The right hand of a man was the one that traditionally carried a weapon, such as a sword or dagger. By presenting the right hand openly, it showed that the man was not carrying a weapon and that he meant no harm to the other man.

Because women did not usually carry weapons, they did not partake in handshaking. The custom has evolved, and handshaking is now common for both sexes. As in ancient times, the modern handshake is a symbol of peace and acceptance, along with equality and openness.

What Is the Big Bang Theory?

For many years, scientists have pondered how the universe was created. The most commonly held theory is the big bang theory. Its premise is that the universe began around 14 billion years ago as a huge dense and hot mass. From this original state, according to certain technical laws and models (Lemaitre's, Hubble's, and Friedmann's, to name a few), the universe has expanded over time.

The theory is based on observations as well as theories, and in 1927 it was first proposed by Georges Lemaitre that the universe began with an enormous explosion of a "primeval atom." In 1929, Edwin Hubble corroborated this when he observed that the galaxies are moving away from Earth in every direction at speeds relative to their distance from Earth.

Further research, based on the measurements of cosmic microwave background and the correlation function of galaxies, led cosmologists to agree that the universe does have a finite age. Improvements in telescopes in recent years have led to findings that also indicate that the universe is expanding. In fact, it appears to be expanding at an accelerating rate. Recent measured abundances of light elements (such as baryons and photons) also suggest that the big bang theory is correct, as it is thought that the abundances could not otherwise exist.

Skeptics of the theory cite three main technical issues for their disbelief: the horizon problem, the flatness problem, and the magnetic monopole problem. Despite this criticism, the big bang theory is now well established in cosmology, and its credibility is thought by many to be limited only by the power of current technology. A number of major Christian churches accept the big bang theory of the creation of the universe.

Is Breakfast Really the Most Important Meal of the Day?

For generations, people have been told that breakfast is the most important meal of the day. Breakfast like a king, lunch like a prince, and dine like a pauper, as the saying goes. But this mandate has been brought into question in recent times, creating a nutritional controversy. So, is breakfast the cornerstone of a healthy diet, or is it an optional morning meal?

Does skipping breakfast make you fatter? While skipping breakfast may make people eat more for lunch, studies have shown that it results in a lower calorie intake over the course of the day. A 2013 study conducted at Cornell University found that college students ate about 145 calories more at lunch when they skipped breakfast, but given that their breakfasts averaged 625 calories, this resulted in a daily saving of 450 calories, as their evening meal usually remained the same regardless of whether breakfast was eaten or not. Another study from the University of Alabama found no difference after sixteen weeks in weight loss between people who were randomly assigned to eat breakfast and people who were randomly assigned to skip it. Despite the common association between skipping breakfast and weight gain, there is no evidence to support this.

Does breakfast kick-start your metabolism? It has long been said that eating breakfast sets a variety of biological processes associated with digestion into motion; that is, breakfast kick-starts your metabolism and makes you lose weight as a result. A 2014 study from the University of Bath in England looked at this issue by monitoring thirty-three volunteers, some who ate breakfast and some who didn't. After six weeks, the resting metabolic rates, cholesterol levels, and blood sugar levels of the subjects were largely unchanged. However, the breakfast-eaters burned around 500 more calories per day in physical activity, but also ate an additional 500 calories each day. So, while eating breakfast provided more energy, the net caloric effect was the same.

Does eating breakfast make you smarter? There is evidence to support the fact that eating breakfast is important for brain development in growing children. In a 2013 study of a group of Chinese kindergarten students that was published in the Elsevier journal *Early Human Development*, it was found that those who regularly ate breakfast had higher IQ scores than those who didn't. These results held even after accounting for other factors, such as their parents' occupations and education.

Does eating breakfast keep the doctor away? A number of 2012 and 2013 studies reported in the *American Journal of Clinical Nutrition* and in *Circulation* found that breakfast-eaters had a lower risk of type 2 diabetes, as well as heart disease. Further study is needed to substantiate these findings, but they do suggest that eating breakfast is beneficial to well-being.

***

The bottom line? Nobody is quite sure. Eating breakfast is unlikely to make you lose weight; however, it may make you inclined to do more exercise but at the same time eat more calories. It may help prevent certain diseases, and it may make your kids smarter. But if you don't like eating breakfast, the scientific evidence that we currently have indicates that you can feel more justified in skipping it.

Why Is Friday the 13th Thought to Be Unlucky?

It is a common superstition in Western society that the thirteenth day of any month is unlucky if it falls on a Friday. An irrationally morbid fear of such a date is known as paraskevidekatriaphobia, deriving from the Greek words *paraskevi* (Friday), *dekatria* (thirteen) and *phobos* (fear).

There is an array of explanations for the origin of the superstition. For instance, it was on Friday, October 13, 1307, that the Grand Master of the Knights Templar and his senior knights were arrested by the king of France, tortured, and killed, while another suggestion has it that it originated from Scandinavia, where twelve feasting gods were joined by Loki, an evil god, and, as a result of his actions, misfortune occurred on Earth. Meanwhile, a common Christian belief of its origins derives from the Last Supper in the Bible, where the traitor Judas was the thirteenth disciple, and Jesus was executed on a Friday.

Despite the origins of the superstition, there is existing evidence suggesting that the date is actually unlucky for some people. Studies have shown that a greater number of car accidents and other sorts of mishaps happen on Friday the 13th than on other Fridays. However, psychologists think that this might be a result of people having an increased sense of anxiety because of the date.

The date also has an effect on society as a whole. For example, it is thought that many people do not travel to work on Friday the 13th because of their fear, while many of the world's office buildings contain no floor thirteen. It is also considered by many to be unlucky for thirteen people to have dinner together.

As mentioned earlier, however, fear of Friday the 13th is a purely Western phenomenon; certain other cultures consider alternate dates to be unlucky.

⁇ What's on the Rags That Villains Use to Make People Pass Out?

A villain sneaks up behind an unsuspecting target, places a rag over their mouth, and almost instantaneously the victim goes weak at the knees and falls to the ground unconscious—we've all seen it many times in movies. But what's on the rag, and is this even possible?

The rag is doused with chloroform, a colorless, sweet-smelling liquid that has been used for its anesthetic properties for years. It was first used in this way by James Young Simpson in 1847, when he administered it to two friends for entertainment purposes. After that, it quickly became a common anesthetic agent.

While it can be used as an anesthetic, the way it is used in the movies is flawed. A chloroform-soaked rag could render a victim unconscious, but it would take far longer than portrayed in fiction. Even with a perfectly measured dose, it would take at least a few minutes. And even then, a continuous volume of chloroform would need to be administered to keep the person under.

There are other issues with the rag method, making it implausible. Chloroform is a highly volatile liquid that loses concentration very rapidly when it is exposed to oxygen. By the time the rag is pressed to the victim's face, it is likely that the chemical would have dissipated and become ineffective.

So, what you see in the movies is completely unrealistic, but let's hope no Hollywood producers read this book. If they do, it might lead to some pretty boring scenes as we sit through five minutes of a villain holding a rag to his victim's face, and then administering more chloroform to make sure it works.

❔ Why Does Sweat Smell?

When people are exposed to heat, through experiencing elevated air temperature, exercise, or emotional stress, they often sweat. The perspiration produced is a healthy and natural part of the body's thermostatic mechanism; when it evaporates from the skin, this process cools the body. However, the degree to which people sweat and the resulting smell that is produced vary greatly.

The skin has two types of sweat glands: eccrine and apocrine. The skin contains millions of eccrine glands, distributed all over the body, and the fluid that they produce consists mainly of salt and water and has no smell. Apocrine glands, meanwhile, tend to be located in areas where there are a lot of hair follicles, such as under the arms, around the genitals and on the head, and the sweat that they produce is fatty. While the sweat from apocrine glands also has no smell, it is a source of nutrition for bacteria on the skin, which break it down, releasing natural chemicals and excrement that produce the unpleasant smell of body odor. This process is particularly noticeable on the feet. Each foot generally contains 250,000 sweat glands and tends to sweat more than other parts of the body. Compounding this are the socks and shoes that provide the feeding bacteria with ideal warm and damp conditions, which also trap the sweat and the resultant odor from the feeding bacteria.

Levels and intensity of body odor vary between different people because some have larger and more active apocrine glands and more aggressive skin bacteria than others. In addition, the nature of the sweat generated by the apocrine glands can be influenced by mood, the consumption of certain foods and drink (such as spicy food, alcohol, and caffeine), the use of drugs, hormone levels, and medical and hereditary conditions.

Body odor from sweat can be reduced by washing regularly with soap, wearing clean clothes, and using a deodorant (which kills bacteria) or antiperspirant (which blocks the pores of the skin, preventing the release of sweat).

How Did the Word "Cocktail" Originate for Some Alcoholic Drinks?

A cocktail is an alcoholic drink with a number of ingredients that are mixed or shaken together. There are hundreds of different concoctions and they are often sweet, colorful, and

interestingly named, such as the Grasshopper, the Rusty Nail, Sex on the Beach, and the Hummingbird.

Like many words and phrases, there are a number of explanations for the origins of the word "cocktail." While it's likely that the correct one will never be known, it's commonly believed that the first written reference to the word was in an 1806 edition of *The Balance, and Columbian Repository*, published in New York, which provided a description of a cocktail.

Some think that the word derived from a drink known as "cock-ale," which in the 18th century was given to anger fighting cocks or to the patrons who attended the cockfights.

Others believe it is a compound deriving from a name for an old American tap (a cock) and the dregs of a barrel (known as the tail). Another explanation is that publicans customarily placed a feather from a cock's tail into alcoholic drinks to warn of their alcoholic content, while yet another is that the word may have come from the French word *coquetel*, which was a mixed drink served to French officers during the American Revolution. It's also said that the name is derived from a particular bar in America where drinks were served out of a ceramic container shaped like a rooster (cock) that had a tap in the tail.

Other theories are that the word derives from a term used in 2nd-century Rome, or from an old medical practice of using a cock's tail to apply throat medicine. There is also a reference to an alcoholic drink being strong enough to "cock the tail" of a bobtailed horse, known as a "cocktailed horse."

Probably the best-known origin story, however, involves an 18th-century innkeeper named Betsy Flanagan who stole chickens from her neighbor and cooked them for her patrons. After the meal, she would mix some drinks and place a feather in each of them. At this display, one French customer yelled in delight, "*Vive le cocktail!*"

Why Did Pirates Make People Walk the Plank Instead of Just Throwing Them Overboard?

According to Hollywood, the standard way to kill anyone on a pirate ship was to make them walk the plank. But given that it would be far quicker to just throw the victim overboard, did this really happen, or is it cinematic sensationalism?

There is some evidence that this barbaric practice did exist. Before his execution in 1769, a seafarer named George Wood confessed to forcing a prisoner to walk the plank. Then, in 1829, the Dutch ship *Vhan Fredericka* was boarded by pirates near the Virgin Islands. The crew members were killed by having cannonballs tied to their feet and being made to walk overboard.

While there are not many other cases that are backed by historical records, the idea gained significant traction with the public in the 1800s, when writers began referring to the practice in literature. Robert Louis Stevenson's 1883 novel *Treasure Island* has a number of references to walking the plank.

It does seem that some pirates did engage in this method of prisoner disposal, but why?

Some say they did it to avoid the murder penalty, the idea being that the prisoner had killed themself. This is highly unlikely, as forcing a person to kill themself would be considered murder, and given that piracy was also a capital crime, what difference did it make, anyway?

Most historians agree that walking the plank was used for two reasons. It was done primarily as a sadistic form of entertainment for the pirates and, secondly, in order to inflict psychological torture on their prisoners, especially in cases where the victim was a disloyal crew member who was guilty of mutiny.

So, while walking the plank did occur, it was relatively rare, and more often than not, the pirates did just throw their victims overboard. So, why does the perverse concept still exist in popular culture today? Maybe it's just too good to drown.

Why Is the *Mona Lisa* Painting So Famous?

Italian Renaissance artist Leonardo da Vinci's painting *La Gioconda*, commonly known as the *Mona Lisa*, is the most famous piece of art in the history of the world and is said to provoke instant recognition almost universally. Many songs have been written about the painting, and it is famous throughout the world. Begun in 1504 and finished in 1515, it is believed to be flawless in its detail and virtually perfect. Even while still in Leonardo's studio in Florence, it was inspiring imitations.

The *Mona Lisa* revolutionized painting. For a start, it was the first portrait that depicted its subject from only the waist up; previous portraits were always full length. Also, the background in the painting is imaginary, describing a line of distant hills, which again was different from previous works in the medium. The depiction of the female subject is extraordinarily vivid and, on seeing it, many have commented that they felt that they were looking at a living person. The smile on the woman is often discussed, with many people seeing it in different ways.

The identity of the painting's female subject is also a matter of debate, some believing her to be the wife of Francesco del Giocondo (hence the painting's Italian name), a rich Florentine silk merchant, while others believe her to be a self-portrait of Leonardo or a construct of his imagination.

In the 1530s, the painting was acquired by the king of France, whereupon it was moved in the 1650s to the Louvre Museum in Paris. Then, from 1800, it hung in Napoleon Bonaparte's bedroom for four years before eventually returning to the museum. In 1911, it was stolen from the Louvre by an employee, who was caught trying to sell it to an art dealer in Florence in 1913, and then in 1956 it was damaged in an acid attack. In 1963, it toured the US, where it was viewed by over a million people, a figure that doubled on its 1974 tour of Tokyo and Moscow.

The momentum of fame, coupled with the painting's colorful history, has made the Mona Lisa increasingly famous. Its current value is estimated as being somewhere in the vicinity of $770 million. The painting now hangs behind glass in the Louvre, where it is viewed by thousands of people every day.

What Is the History of the Pizza?

The pizza, in one form or another, has been around for thousands of years. Some claim it is based on pita bread, eaten in the Middle East. Some say that its origin stems from flatbreads, resembling the modern-day focaccia, which were eaten in ancient times around the Mediterranean. Archaeologists have uncovered structures resembling pizzerias in the remains of Pompeii, which was destroyed in AD 79 by the eruption of Mount Vesuvius. Evidence also suggests that the Greeks brought pizza to Italy in the 1st century AD. Flat baked breads covered in dressings were also said to be eaten in Rome in 300 BC.

The word *pizza*, meaning "pie," first appeared near Naples and Rome in AD 1000, and it is often accepted that Naples is the birthplace of the modern-day pizza, with the Neapolitan being the original pizza. The first modern-day pizzeria, which is still in existence, was opened in Naples by Raffaele Esposito in 1830. Pizza was considered food for the poor person, but to honor a visit by King Umberto I and Queen Margherita of Italy, Esposito created a special pizza resembling the Italian flag. The queen was impressed and the Margherita pizza was born.

The pizza was brought from Naples to the United States in 1897 by Gennaro Lombardi, who opened a general store in New York that sold pizza. The pizzas became so popular that he opened the first American pizzeria in 1905. Called Lombardi's, the shop still operates today.

In the early 1900s in the United States, pizza was eaten predominantly by immigrant Italians. During World War II, American troops in Italy ate pizza extensively. When they returned, pizza became popular throughout the United States. Pizza shops began opening in the 1950s, and the trend spread quickly. Today, pizza is an international food.

Why Are Male Birds More Colorful Than Female Birds?

In the vast majority of bird species, the male parades around looking regal with brightly colored plumage, while the female's feathers are dull and drab in comparison. It hardly seems fair, but there is a scientific explanation for this ornithological phenomenon.

Charles Darwin developed much of the theory that explains the differences in birds. He proposed that in animals where the males must compete for mates, certain characteristics that are unique to the males are propagated because of sexual selection. These features are either weapons that allow the males to fight for the females, such as the horns on a buffalo, or ornaments that attract the attention of the females, such as colorful feathers in birds.

Female birds see the brightness of the male as an important indicator of his health. A colorful male is a strong and healthy one, better able to acquire plentiful food for them both, as well as for any chicks. This has been proven in a number of instances. In the house finch, the brightness of the male is directly related to the pigments obtained from high-quality seed. Brighter birds of other species have also been shown to be better at providing food for females than their duller counterparts.

Color in male birds is also used as a defense when fighting other males for territory. As color indicates health and strength, a brightly colored male is more likely to scare his opponents away. With the red-winged black bird, scientists have found that when the male's wings are artificially dyed completely black, the bird is more likely to lose his territory.

Female birds are usually less colorful for a reason, too. When nesting, they are more at risk of being attacked by predators, so a bland appearance allows them to blend in with their surroundings.

However, where gender roles are reversed and the male incubates the eggs while the female defends the territory and fights for access to the males, the female bird has the more colorful plumage. Sandpipers, phalaropes, and button quail are examples of this.

❓ Why Do Most Car Accidents Happen Close to Home?

Various studies have found that around half of all car accidents occur five miles or less from home, and over three quarters of accidents happen 15 miles or less from home. Obviously, a higher percentage of driving is done close to home, but is there any other reason for these disproportionately high figures?

Most experts agree that the main reason we have so many accidents near home is that we're driving in our comfort zone. We feel relaxed because of the repetitiveness of the drive and the familiarity of our local area, and, quite simply, we don't concentrate as much. We know the roads, the turns, the intersections, and the landmarks all so well that sometimes when we arrive home, we can't even remember the drive. It's as if we're on autopilot and we don't focus on the complicated task of driving.

The problem with this approach is that accidents often happen because of unpredictable events, like the bad driving of another, an animal crossing the road, or a mechanical failure. Vigilance is still needed to deal with these issues, and because we lack it when we're near home, more accidents happen.

We are also more likely to be distracted when we're close to home. We sometimes don't put on the seat belt if we're just going to a nearby store, and we're more likely to talk on a cell phone or scan the radio for music.

On a long drive out of town, however, people tend to be more concerned about safety issues, and this makes them concentrate on their driving. Highway driving is usually on straight roads as well, with fewer obstacles and turns, so the number of accidents per hour of driving is reduced. But as we approach home after a long trip, we often relax as we enter our familiar territory, and that's when problems are more likely to arise.

There is one consolation with all of this. While the vast majority of accidents do happen close to home, they tend to be relatively minor, only resulting in small bumps and scrapes.

 What Makes Drugs Addictive?

Drug addiction is the dependence on a substance to the point where the user feels that they must have the drug, regardless of consequences. Addiction varies from drug to drug. Compared with alcohol, it generally takes far fewer uses of heroin to become addicted. Drug addiction also varies from person to person, and some people are genetically predisposed to it. The most common drug addictions are to alcohol, caffeine, and nicotine.

The addiction to drugs can be physical, psychological, or both. Physical dependency means the chemistry of the addict is altered so that they must have the drug or suffer symptoms of withdrawal. Without the drug, the addict might feel physically ill. Psychological dependency occurs when the person relies on the drug emotionally and craves it for feelings of reward. Without the drug, the addict might feel stressed or fearful, so they keep taking it to feel good.

Scientists believe that certain drugs (including cocaine and amphetamines) stimulate particular areas of the brain to release large amounts of dopamine, a chemical that occurs naturally in the brain and produces a feeling of euphoria. Other drugs (including alcohol) mimic endorphins, which have an effect that is similar to that of dopamine, and produce euphoria. After prolonged exposure to either type of drug, a craving for this feeling of euphoria can come to dominate the person's thoughts, and a physical or psychological dependency is the result.

Once the euphoria associated with a drug has passed, a protein is produced in the brain that inhibits the release of dopamine. This can leave the drug user depressed and unable to derive pleasure from previously enjoyable activities. This generally leads to the person taking the drug again to feel "normal," often in larger doses because of the built-up level of tolerance. And so the cycle continues and the dependency increases.

How Do Martial Artists Break Things with Their Bare Hands?

For years, martial artists have demonstrated their ability to break multiple bricks or planks of wood by striking the dense objects with their bare hands. This seemingly superhuman ability has led some to question whether a trick or illusion is involved. In fact, the seemingly supernatural skill is mastered purely by training and technique.

Martial arts students are trained to break small objects early on in their careers. As they practice for long periods, they create tiny fractures in the bones of the hands, which heal with additional calcium deposits. This enlarges and strengthens the hands, making them more able to break larger objects, and reducing the chance of injury.

It is the amount of force that is applied that breaks the object. To create force, the martial artist must create as much hand speed as possible. The greater the speed of the hand, the more likely that the break will be successful. Studies show that maximum hand speed is achieved when the arm is about 80 percent extended. One of the main techniques used to hit the object at this maximum speed is to focus beyond the object, as if you were trying to hit a few inches past it. This ensures that the hand does not decelerate prior to contact with the target. To ensure high speed, it is also important to relax, as tension can make the body stiffen and so produce less speed. Some say the hand should be pulled back quickly after the strike, which provides a faster, whip-like technique, like a snake biting.

Although immense skill and technique are involved, the boards or bricks are usually not stacked together but are separated by pencils. This means that they are broken one at a time, instead of as a block. Also, the boards are struck parallel to the grain so that they are easier to break.

⁇ What Is the Origin of Halloween?

Halloween falls on October 31 and is celebrated in much of the Western world. It usually involves children dressing up in costumes and knocking on doors in a ritual known as trick-or-treating. The theme of the night is ghosts, witches, and magic, with black cats, goblins, and candles in pumpkins being the prominent symbols.

Halloween's origin dates back to the pagan Celtic festival of Samhain. More than two thousand years ago, the Celts celebrated their new year on November 1. That day marked the end of the harvest and the beginning of the long winter, a time when death ran rife. The Celts believed that on the night before the new year began, the ghosts of the dead returned to Earth. The harvest festival began on October 31. Fires were lit and sacrifices of animals, crops, and even humans were offered to their gods. Those at the festival wore costumes and masks in an attempt to ward off evil spirits. An ember from the fire was given to each family on November 1 to take home for a new fire. This was thought to keep homes free from evil spirits throughout the winter.

When the Romans conquered the Celtic lands, they combined two of their festivals with the festival of Samhain. One was the festival in honor of Pomona, the goddess of fruit and trees, and the other was Feralia, a day in February when they honored the dead. By AD 800, Christianity had spread, and Pope Boniface IV made November 1 the day to honor saints and martyrs. It was All Saints' Day, also called All Hallows' Day, from All Hallowed Souls. The night before was known as All Hallows' Eve, which was eventually contracted to Halloween.

Trick-or-treating is thought to have originated with the European custom of "souling" in the AD 800s. On All Souls' Day on November 2, beggars would walk from village to village, begging for bread with currants, known as soul cakes. In return for the cakes, the beggars would say prayers for the person's dead relatives, which were thought to assist the dead soul's passage to heaven.

Irish immigrants brought the custom of Halloween to America in the 1840s.

How Do Steroids Enhance Sports Performance?

Drugs in sports have been a hot topic for more than 25 years. In particular, the use of anabolic steroids is highly contentious, especially after the high-profile banning of Ben Johnson after he won the gold medal for the 100-meter race in the 1988 Olympics. The use of steroids in sports also received much publicity with the cyclist Lance Armstrong's controversy.

Many athletes and medical professionals believe that the use of steroids enhances performance. Anabolic steroids are synthetic compounds whose structure is similar to the male sex hormone testosterone. This hormone has an anabolic effect on the body; that is, it increases the growth of muscular and skeletal tissue. It also has an androgenic effect, which results in an increase in male sexual characteristics. Anabolic steroids bind to hormone receptors and stimulate the synthesis of certain enzymes, which increase phosphocreatine synthesis and protein synthesis. Phosphocreatine synthesis allows athletes to train harder and longer, while protein synthesis helps them to increase muscle mass. Steroids also stimulate bone marrow and increase the production of red blood cells. A large intake of protein by athletes is also essential to increase the muscle mass. Without the use of anabolic steroids, muscles build up slowly, but steroids reverse the short-term catabolic effect, promoting nitrogen retention, and this also helps build muscle mass quickly.

Apart from the increase in power from added muscle bulk, and the ability to train more, steroids can help to enhance performance in other ways. The increase in male hormones in the body increases aggression and motivation, which can positively affect training and performance. The use of steroids is also thought by some to have a positive psychological effect on performance.

Some experts claim that steroids do not enhance performance; a number of studies have been inconclusive on this point. Despite this difference of opinion, there is an array of incontrovertible side effects from anabolic steroid use. High blood pressure, stress, aggression, severe acne, and sexual dysfunction are some of them. In extreme cases, steroid use is thought to lead to brain cancer.

How Do Animals Hibernate?

Hibernation allows certain animals to conserve energy and sleep through the winter months. Most animals choose a secluded place to hibernate, such as a cave or burrow. Some animals awaken periodically and eat food they have stored, while others sleep for a whole season. The reason animals hibernate is to survive the cold weather and lack of food in the winter.

During hibernation, the metabolism of an animal is reduced to a very low level, along with the breathing rate and heart rate. Also, the body temperature is reduced (to a level that can match the ambient temperature). During this time, the animal gradually uses up fat stores for energy. When asleep, an animal moves and has an active brain, whereas with true hibernation the animal appears dead and can even be touched without being aware of it.

To prepare for hibernation, most animals eat a lot of food so that they can store fat deposits to help them survive the winter. The animals use these fat stores and do not lose any muscle bulk. This means they come out of hibernation with the strength they need to hunt.

Both land and aquatic animals hibernate, including mice, bats, frogs, snakes, and squirrels. Cold-blooded animals hibernate when cold weather causes their body temperatures to drop. Bears are popularly depicted as hibernating in winter, but they are not true hibernators. At this time of year, the heart rate of a bear slows, but the body temperature remains fairly constant, and the bear can be easily roused.

By giving them hydrogen sulfide, scientists have artificially induced hibernation in mice. This raises the possibility of inducing hibernation in other animals, including humans.

Why Don't Birds Fall Off Branches When Asleep?

People often wonder why birds don't fall from a perch when they go to sleep.

Birds' feet prevent them from falling. Their feet are similar to our hands, although they generally have three toes fanned forward and one pointing to the rear.

Many birds' feet can do an array of tasks, including walking, hopping, and holding on to objects. The sharp claws and long toes of birds allow them to balance in a multitude of positions and cling to rough surfaces.

When a bird lands on a branch, its opposing toes wrap around the branch tightly. The muscles in the bird's legs contain long tendons, and when the bird clasps a branch, the tendons tighten and the toes lock. This involuntary reflex fastens the bird to the branch. The more the bird bends its legs, the greater the pull on the tendons and the firmer the grip on the branch. Once the feet are locked on to the branch, the bird can safely sleep without risking falling off.

To release its grasp, the bird stands up and straightens its legs. This releases the tendons. It actually takes less effort for a bird to stay on a branch than to let go.

Is the Human Body Really 80 Percent Water?

It is often stated in health magazines that 80 percent of the human body is water. But is this actually true?

The human body depends on water. The amount of fluids in the body strongly influences a person's well-being. Although the exact percentage of water varies, depending on what source is quoted, scientists believe that we are in fact made up of around 72 percent water and 8 percent chemical compounds. The remaining 20 percent is bone and solid tissue. The water actually contains sodium chloride (salt) and potassium chloride, and about two-thirds of it is in our cells. The rest is free-flowing liquid in the form of blood plasma and liquid between the cells.

Water plays a vital role in maintaining all of the body's systems and also in repairing any damage to the body. Blood is more than 83 percent water, and in order for it to properly carry out its life-preserving functions, the body must be sufficiently hydrated. The brain, which controls every aspect of the body, is more than 80 percent water. The fluid inside the nerves is also made up of water and minerals.

Water also has a large impact on our energy. The liver uses water to metabolize fat into usable energy. Drinking a lot of water speeds up the metabolism and results in increased strength and energy. A drop of 5 percent in body fluids causes a 30 percent drop in energy, and a 15 percent drop in body fluids causes death. Water is also important in keeping the temperature of the body constant.

Because so much of the body is water, it is advisable to drink a large amount of high-quality water to stay healthy. About 2 liters per day is recommended, depending on factors such as the ambient temperature and humidity and a person's level of activity.

Why Is the Bermuda Triangle Such a Feared Boating Area?

The Bermuda Triangle is an area of about 1.5 million square miles in the Atlantic Ocean that is situated between Bermuda, Puerto Rico, and the tip of Florida. It is famous because of the supposedly inordinate number of unexplained boat and plane disappearances in the region. The suspicious circumstances under which vessels have disappeared have led some to believe that the Bermuda Triangle, also known as the Devil's Triangle, possesses paranormal forces that violate the laws of physics.

The Bermuda Triangle found fame in the 1950s when a number of "mysterious disappearances" were reported. It was then highly publicized in the 1974 book *The Bermuda Triangle* by Charles Berlitz, which described several inexplicable events, including the 1945 loss of a squadron of five navy aircraft, known as Flight 19. To add to the mysticism, the US Navy ascribed the loss to unknown causes. The book prompted many theories, both natural and supernatural.

Some experts attribute the phenomenon to the amount of methane hydrates in the area's continental shelves. It is said that methane eruptions are capable of producing enormous bubbles that can sink ships. Some say the amount of gas in the water can dramatically affect buoyancy, causing ships to sink without warning. The methane gas in the atmosphere is also said to make the air less dense, causing planes to lose lift and crash. Less dense air also interrupts the altimeters on planes, giving the impression that the plane is climbing, which can result in the plane diving and crashing. Others say that freak waves in the area can cause ships to sink, and the high electromagnetic activity there can cause problems with electronic equipment. Unpredictable weather patterns and the turbulent Gulf Stream waters are also cited as explanations.

The US Coast Guard, however, does not recognize the Bermuda Triangle as an exceptional area, remarking that the incidence of lost ships and planes is no greater there than in any other heavily traversed area. It chalks up the disappearances to human error, including a lack of local knowledge and poor sea and navigational skills. Major insurance companies do not charge greater insurance premiums for travel in the area.

Can Babies Hear Voices While inside the Womb?

It has long been suggested that babies can hear voices and music while they are still in the womb, and for years now some mothers have been known to talk to their unborn children and play them music.

A number of studies have now been carried out to test this theory, including one that involved recording sounds picked up by the inner ears of unborn sheep. These studies found that the womb dampens most sounds, except those with low frequencies; high-pitched sounds are muffled. The researchers concluded that deep vowel sounds are likely to be heard but that high-pitched consonants will most likely be inaudible. Music containing a lot of bass is therefore more likely to be heard than classical music.

The researchers further concluded that, while unborn children could probably hear the melody of speech, the definition of individual words would be too muffled to hear. Fetuses younger than thirty weeks were found not to respond to any sounds at all.

The ears of fetuses are filled with water, so they hear via vibrations in their skulls. This makes the mother's voice the most heard sound in the womb, because it vibrates to the baby. This is thought to shape the development of the child to recognize and prefer its native tongue and its mother's voice. It is also believed that babies can recognize music that they heard regularly before they were born. However, no evidence has been found to support the suggestion that certain voices or types of music enhance a child's intelligence.

 ## How Did Chopsticks Originate?

Chopsticks are the traditional eating utensils of most of Asia. They are a pair of sticks, equal in length, that are held in one hand and used to pick up food. They can be made of wood, bamboo, bone, ivory, metal, or plastic. Some say that silver chopsticks were used by Chinese royalty to detect poison in the food. Poison would react with the silver, turning it black.

The term "chopsticks" comes from the Chinese Pidgin English word *chop*, meaning "quick." The Mandarin word for chopsticks is *kuàizi*, which means "the bamboo objects for eating quickly."

It is thought that chopsticks were developed in China around five thousand years ago. Food was cooked in large pots, and people would break off twigs to retrieve the food from the pot. As the population of China grew rapidly, resources became scarce, and food was cut into small pieces so that it would cook faster and less fuel would be consumed.  These small cuts of food eliminated the need for knives, and chopsticks came to be used for the whole meal. Confucius also perpetuated the use of chopsticks by dissuading people from having knives at the table. He was a vegetarian and associated knives with slaughterhouses.

By AD 500, chopsticks had spread to Korea, Vietnam, and Japan. Originally used in Japan only for religious ceremonies, they quickly became popular and widespread.

Many Asians believe that the use of chopsticks improves the memory, learning skills, and dexterity. Some superstitions surround chopsticks. It is thought that a person eating with an uneven pair of chopsticks will miss the next boat, plane, or train. Dropping chopsticks is considered a sign of bad luck to come.

Why Do Fingers Wrinkle in Water?

A bather who is in the water for a long time will note that their fingers and toes turn wrinkly.

The human skin is covered with a special oil called sebum. It is not visible to the naked eye but is produced by the epidermis, the outermost layer of skin. Sebum is the reason we leave oily fingerprints on the objects we touch. It moistens, lubricates, and protects the skin. It also acts to waterproof the skin. Sebum is the reason that water runs off the skin instead of soaking in.

After a long time in the water, the layer of sebum gets washed away, allowing the water to penetrate the skin. This leaves the skin waterlogged, causing it to swell in some places but not others. This gives the skin its wrinkly appearance. The condition is most noticeable on the feet and hands, where the skin is thickest.

After the bather leaves the water, the absorbed water quickly evaporates, and the wrinkles on the fingers disappear. The skin returns to normal and develops a new coating of protective sebum.

Is There Any Science to Déjà Vu?

Déjà vu is when a person gets a strong feeling that what they're currently experiencing has happened to them before, even though they know it hasn't. It is a French phrase that translates as "already seen," and was coined by the French scientist Émile Boirac in 1876. Around 70 percent of people admit to having experienced déjà vu, yet it is a little understood phenomenon with over forty theories to explain it, ranging from reincarnation to the existence of multiple universes.

The most cogent theories are memory-based and dream-based.

Some scientists believe that déjà vu involves an anomaly of the memory that can occur when information that was learned but later forgotten is still stored in the brain. When the person experiences similar occurrences, latent memories are triggered. This gives a feeling of familiarity, but it is not familiar enough that you can connect the present to something you've experienced before. This may happen when you see something you have seen before, either in real life or on television or in a photo, but just don't remember it.

The dream-based explanation is of a similar ilk. This theory is that a person may have dreamed about a similar situation or place to the one currently being experienced. The person cannot remember the dream, but it is invoked by the real situation, leading to an eerie sense of familiarity.

It is easy to see how some people attribute déjà vu to paranormal or extrasensory forces, but it's almost certainly related to the internal workings of our brains—scientists just can't explain exactly how.

Can a Chicken Run with Its Head Cut Off?

The expression "running around like a chicken with its head cut off" refers to someone in a frenzy. The colorful saying prompts many to wonder whether a chicken can actually keep moving once its head has been separated from its body.

It is true that a decapitated chicken can run around for a while. Although the brain is severed from the spinal cord, precluding any voluntary control of movement, electrical impulses from the spinal cord can still cause the chicken to flap its wings and even run. Adrenaline still present in the chicken's muscles also allows this to happen for a short while.

Any such movement by a chicken will usually last for only up to a minute. But in 1945, the locomotion of a chicken in Colorado named Mike lasted a lot longer. In trying to butcher the bird, its owner cut off the chicken's head, but the brain stem was left intact. Without a head, Mike was able to balance on a perch and even walk. Mike was fed with an eyedropper, although he would often choke, and his owner would clear the obstruction with a syringe. Mike was taken to shows where people paid to view him. In 1947, he choked and died. It was later determined that the ax had missed Mike's jugular vein and a blood clot had formed that prevented him from bleeding to death. His intact brain stem allowed his reflexes to operate, which accounted for his movement.

 ## Why Do People Get Goose Bumps?

Nearly everyone gets goose bumps from time to time, usually when they are cold, apprehensive, or afraid. Goose bumps are an automatic emotional or physical response that we normally can't control.

Also known as *cutes anserinae*, goose bumps are the tiny lumps that appear on a person's skin at the base of the hairs. They are caused by a reflex called piloerection and are named after the skin of a plucked goose. Piloerection occurs when the muscles at the base of each hair contract and pull the hair erect. The piloerection reflex is governed by the sympathetic nervous system, which is responsible for the fight-or-flight reaction.

Once a particular stimulus occurs, nerves discharge, causing the muscles to contract and the hairs to stand on end.

Goose bumps also occur in other animals and are responsible for making cold animals warm and scared animals more impressive looking. When the hairs stand on end, the body is more insulated against the cold because a layer of air becomes trapped under the hairs. An animal will also appear larger and more intimidating to enemies when its hairs stand erect. An example is the porcupine, whose quills stand on end when it is threatened. Some experts believe that goose bumps also provide additional blood to the muscles to assist with the fight-or-flight reaction.

Humans now have minimal body hair, so goose bumps serve no known purpose. They are a vestigial trait from the days of our hair-covered ancestors.

Has Any Human Been Successfully Raised by Animals?

In the world of literature, several fictional characters have been raised by animals, most notably Tarzan, in a series of novels by Edgar Rice Burroughs, and Mowgli, from Rudyard Kipling's *Jungle Book* series.

In real life, there have been around a hundred instances of children being raised by or living with animals due to being abandoned or lost in the wild.

The first famous such child was Peter the Wild Boy, who was found in Hanover, Germany, in 1724 at the age of 12. When he was found, he walked on all fours, climbed trees, and ate plants, and he never learned to speak. Without human contact at a young age, children often have difficulty mastering language and fitting into society. Other, less documented examples are the Hessian wolf-children, found in 1341; the Lithuanian bear-boys, discovered in the 1600s; and the young girls Kamala and Amala, who were discovered in 1920 and said to have been raised by wolves in India.

A more recent case was Oxana Malaya, who was born in 1983 and found at the age of eight in Ukraine. Because Oxana's alcoholic parents could not care for her adequately, she had lived in a kennel behind her house with a pack of dogs for most of her young life. She had been cared for by the dogs and developed dog-like mannerisms and behavioral patterns. She crouched, barked, and growled, as well as smelled her food before eating it. She had extremely acute senses of hearing, sight, and smell. After she was discovered, she lived in a facility for disabled people, where she found social interaction and learning language skills very difficult.

These remarkable accounts illustrate that it is possible for animals to raise and care for people in a manner similar to the story of Tarzan.

Why Do Men Have Nipples?

Once a human embryo has been conceived, no matter what its ultimate gender, it follows a female template, adopting all female characteristics, including nipples. After a number of weeks in this state, a certain gene in the male embryo stimulates the production of the male hormone testosterone, which prompts the embryo to develop masculine qualities. While the nipples remain present (because they are formed before this process

48

takes place), they will not function in the way that they would have had the embryo been supplied with female hormones.

Not only do male babies have nipples, but they are also born with breast tissue and milk ducts and glands. These are normally inoperative, but, if men experience increased levels of the female hormone estrogen and a lack of testosterone, they can develop breasts like those of women and, in extreme cases, even perform lactation. Because men have breast tissue, they are at risk from breast cancer, albeit to a far lesser extent than women are.

It is thought by some that men might once have used nipples to help feed their young during lean times. Now that this no longer occurs, it has been asked of scientists why evolution has not done away with these superfluous male nipples. The common response is that, because diseases affecting the nipples are rare in men, there is no genetic imperative to do away with the nipples, and so they simply remain.

Why Are So Many Barns in America Red?

In the rural areas of the United States, nearly all farms have barns to house animals, machinery, or feed for stock. Many of these barns, particularly in New England and New York state, are painted red. Some wonder about this uniformity of color.

In the 1800s, when a great number of barns were built, many rural families were poor. Painting for aesthetics was considered a luxury, but painting was often necessary to protect wood from the elements.

At the time, ferric oxide was one of the cheapest and most readily available chemicals for farmers. Ferric oxide was red and early American farmers used it to make their own paint. When the ferric oxide was mixed with other ingredients, such as milk, lime, and linseed oil, the presence of this chemical yielded a red paint. It was this paint that was used on the barns.

Many modern-day barns are painted red, continuing the tradition. In some poorer areas, such as parts of the South, barns are often left unpainted. More affluent areas, which raise horses and purebred livestock, have barns of yellow, white, or green. Farms with barns of these colors are often found in Virginia, Kentucky, and Pennsylvania.

How Do Bees Navigate?

For years, scientists have studied how bees get around. Typically, a bee travels in an irregular path to a food source (which may be up to 6 miles away) and then returns to the hive in a straight line. After the bee performs a dance (a circular pattern with an occasional zigzag) at the hive, other bees make their way to that food source in a straight line.

Studies show that bees are adept learners. If a particular plant produces nectar, a bee will return to it, ignoring other, less nourishing plants. An experiment in which bees were trained to negotiate a maze indicated their learning abilities. Although most experts agree that bees are able to learn, there is much conjecture as to how bees find their way and the relevance of their peculiar dances.

Some argue that bees use odor and their acute sense of smell, as well as various landmarks on their route, to guide them. They say that the dance alerts the remaining bees to the particular odor, which they then follow to the source. Others believe that bees possess a map-like spatial memory, which they use to navigate.

Most experts now agree that bees use the sun as a reference point when navigating. It is thought that bees use the sun as a relatively stationary point and orient themselves by maintaining a fixed angle relative to the sun. These experts believe that the dance performed by a bee directs the other bees to the food by reference to the sun, indicating the angle relative to the sun that the other bees should follow.

❓ Why Do Whales Beach Themselves?

The phenomenon of whales beaching themselves, either singly or in large groups, has long been a scientific mystery. Sometimes beached whales—especially large ones—are already dead and simply wash up on shore, although in many cases, beached whales are alive. The reason for this behavior is still unclear. When beached, whales often die of dehydration, drown when high tides cover their blowholes or suffocate under their own weight.

The species of whales that beach themselves alive swim in large pods. Pilot whales, which have a tendency to strand themselves en masse, have a complex social structure and exhibit extreme loyalty to members of the group that are in trouble. It is thought that, if the lead pilot whale becomes disoriented or sick, and unable to keep itself at the surface to breathe, it might swim ashore. The rest of the group will then follow it as a response to its distress call, or out of loyalty, only to suffer the same fate.

It is also believed that whales use the Earth's magnetic field, combined with an awareness of coastal topography, to navigate.

In places where these factors are abnormal, whales might become disoriented and think that the water is deeper than it is. Lending weight to this theory is the fact that whales are often found stranded in the same place and, if towed back into the water, typically strand themselves again on the same beach.

Whales are often found stranded where the beach slopes away gradually, which has led some to believe that, in such places, the sonar system used by whales to measure distance has nothing to bounce back from, giving the whale the impression that deep water lies ahead. Others believe that whales chase their prey into shallow waters before getting stranded by the ebbing tide.

Another theory is that underwater sonar used by navies and noises emitted during seismic testing for oil and gas are so intense that whales are forced to surface too quickly. The resulting rapid change in pressure can cause decompression sickness or hemorrhaging in their ears, which can confuse them or inhibit their navigational abilities, causing them to become beached.

Can Holding in a Fart Kill You?

Flatulence, colloquially known as farting, is considered taboo in most social settings, particularly if accompanied by an unpleasant odor or noise. This unacceptability makes many feel compelled to hold in any gas. This has led some to ask whether this retention of flatulence is harmful.

For centuries, it has been believed that retaining flatulence could be dangerous. The Roman emperor Claudius even passed a law legalizing flatulence at banquets because of health concerns. At the time, the widespread opinion was that a person could be poisoned if gas was not emitted immediately.

Flatulence is a mixture of gases that are produced by bacteria and yeasts in the intestinal tract and released through the anus. Most animals and all mammals flatulate, with the average person releasing up to a third of a gallon of gas per day. The gas consists primarily of oxygen, nitrogen, carbon dioxide, hydrogen, and methane. The presence of sulfuric components is responsible for the common odor.

These gases that constitute flatulence are not harmful to human health and are a natural aspect of the intestinal contents. They are not in any way poisonous, and no particular harm can result from holding in flatulence. The main side effect of this retentive practice is the discomfort of a stomachache from the buildup of gas pressure in the intestines. Some medical professionals claim that in extreme circumstances, this practice can result in a distension of the bowel, potentially leading to constipation.

Does Shaved Hair Grow Back Thicker and Darker?

It's often said that cutting or shaving hair on the head or body makes it grow back faster, thicker and darker than it originally was. This is not true.

The amount of hair on the human body, as well as its growth rate and color, are determined by the individual hair follicles. These aren't affected or stimulated by shaving, nor does shaving promote the growth of additional hair follicles. The diameter of the hair follicles is also unaffected. In fact, the thickness and darkness of an individual's hair, as well as its growth rate, are determined by genetics. The live part of the hair is actually underneath the skin, in the follicle, and so shaving or cutting has no impact on it.

The myth that hair grows back thicker and darker after shaving probably stems from the fact that the shorter hair at the early stages of regrowth seems tougher than longer hair. This is due to the fact that each hair is usually thicker at the base, where it has been cut, than the ends, which taper off naturally. This makes the hair blunter and more noticeable than the original hair, which had a much finer tip. In time, the cut hair will grow to be the same thickness and density as it was at its previous length.

What Makes Chili Peppers Hot?

The chili pepper is native to Mexico, where it has been used for thousands of years—some estimate since 7500 BC. When Christopher Columbus landed in the islands of the Caribbean, indigenous people had long been using and growing chili peppers. Columbus took some back to Spain, however, and from there, they quickly spread to the rest of the world. Belonging to the same family as tomatoes and potatoes, chili peppers vary in shape, size, and texture, and their colors range from green to orange to red. The heat of different chili peppers also varies, and the color of the chili is not necessarily indicative of its heat.

An alkaloid substance called capsaicin, along with four related chemicals, known as capsaicinoids, are responsible for the chili's distinctive hot, peppery taste. These chemicals are contained predominantly in the chili membrane to which the seeds are attached. Each capsaicinoid has a different effect on the mouth, generally stimulating the nerve receptors in the tongue and skin that sense heat and pain. If consumed to excess, capsaicin causes painful inflammation and even burns the skin.

The heat of chili peppers is measured in Scoville units (named after Wilbur Scoville, who developed the scale). The number of Scoville units indicates the amount of capsaicin present. Jalapeños generally average around 4,000 units, while one of the hottest chilis, the *naga jolokia* from India, measures 855,000 units.

Scientists believe the reason chili peppers are hot is to repel mammals but not birds. Chili seeds pass straight through the digestive system of a bird, which helps disperse the seeds to grow new plants. However, the seeds do not pass through mammals. It is thought that chili peppers evolved to be hot so that mammals would not eat them, as that would hinder the spread of the seeds.

To mitigate the effects of eating a hot chili, some recommend ingesting salt, yogurt, mint leaves, cucumber, or milk. Drinking water often exacerbates the heat.

❓ Why Do People Open Their Mouths When Applying Mascara?

If you've applied mascara, or watched it being applied, you've probably wondered the same thing: Why on earth do people open their mouths while doing it?

There are a number of theories as to why this peculiar phenomenon occurs, including the following:

- Keeping your mouth shut requires effort. When you're relaxed or concentrating on a delicate task, the neck muscles slacken and the mouth opens spontaneously. Many people don't even know it's happening.

- Having the mouth open in an "O" shape temporarily stops a person from blinking, which is preferable when applying mascara.

- The mouth muscles are used to help move the facial muscles in order to get at the different lashes, particularly the more difficult corner lashes.

- When the mouth is opened, the eyes naturally open wider, making it easier to apply the mascara.

- Opening the mouth stretches out the skin around the eyes. This helps to keep the skin farther away from the lashes so the mascara doesn't smudge on the skin.

- It is an unconscious and involuntary response that occurs when someone is concentrating, similar to how people sometimes stick out their tongues when doing another task.

- There is no reason at all. Humans are strange and will never be fully understood.

Now, go on to the next question, and stop moving your mouth around to test these theories.

Why Do Fast-Moving Wheels Appear to Go Backward on Film?

Often in movies and on television, the spoked wheels of a vehicle appear to rotate backward. This is known as the reverse rotation effect, or the wagon-wheel effect, because it was originally noticed with the spokes of wagon wheels.

It is actually an optical illusion caused by an intermittent display or recording system. Movie and television cameras generally operate at between 24 and 30 frames per second—that is, they flash on and off that many times per second. Because of the speed, the eyes can't see the separate film frames, and the brain perceives the film as continuous. If the spokes of a wheel rotate at a multiple of the same number of frames per second, they will appear to be in the same exact position every time the shutter opens. This makes them seem motionless. However, if the wheel slows down slightly, the spokes of the wheel do not have time to rotate to the same position before the shutter opens again. Consequently, the spokes of the wheel appear to be rotating backward.

This same effect can be seen in films of helicopter rotors and aircraft propellers, and can also occur if lighting is temporally modulated, such as with strobe lighting. When an alternating current is used, light flickers at an increased rate and can cause the same effect. But some studies report that people can see the reverse rotation effect with a wheel illuminated by continuous light in real conditions. This has led to a theory that, like movies, human vision is a series of still frames, which are perceived to be continuous. These studies suggest that this effect is generally seen in real life only after prolonged gazing.

Why Do People's Eyes Sometimes Appear Red in Photographs?

Much to the chagrin of photographers, when a photo is taken with a flash at night, the eyes of the subject of the photo might appear bright red.

This is because the flash goes off before the pupil has time to close, resulting in the red-eye effect. As a result, the flash is focused by the lens of the eye on the retina at the back of the eye. The retina is covered with tiny blood vessels, and these red vessels are focused by the lens of the eye back to the camera. This makes the eyes in the photograph appear red.

The more open the pupils are, the greater the red-eye effect, because more of the illuminated retina can be seen. The effect is also generally more pronounced in people with light eye color and also in children, whose eyes tend to be lighter. This is because pale irises have less melanin in them and allow more light to pass through to the retina.

The red-eye effect also occurs in other animals, such as cats, which have a light-reflecting layer behind the retina that acts to improve night vision. This layer also increases the red-eye effect, although the color reflected can vary from animal to animal.

The red-eye effect can be reduced by using a bounce flash, which is aimed at a nearby wall so that it enters the eye at a different angle, or by using a special camera that employs a series of low-level flashes before the main flash fires. This allows the iris to contract, thereby reducing the effect. Increasing the lighting in a room so that the pupils are not as dilated also reduces the effect.

❓ Is There Any Science to Palm Reading?

Palm reading is a practice used by fortune-tellers to perceive the character, fortune, and future of a person by studying that individual's palm. It is also known as chiromancy (from the Greek words *kheir* meaning "hand" and *manteia* meaning "divination") and derives originally from Greek mythology.

People's hands are like fingerprints: no two are identical. A fortune-teller "reads" a person's palm by interpreting the different lines and "mounts" (which are rises or ridges) on the hand, which supposedly reveal things about them.

There are three main lines on the hand. The heart line is the top line across the hand. It supposedly indicates a person's emotional feelings, such as depression or happiness, as well as a person's romantic situation and the physical well-being of their heart. The head line is the next line down, and it runs across the middle of the palm. This line represents a person's intelligence, creativity, and communication style. The life line is

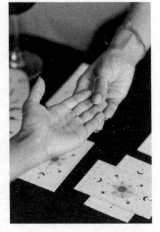

the next major line. It arcs from the left of the left palm and down to the wrist. This line indicates a person's health and general well-being. It is also said to indicate any major life changes although, contrary to popular belief, its length is unrelated to the length of a person's life.

There are other lines, including the simian crease, the fate line, and the sun, union, Mercury, and travel lines. These are said to indicate an array of things, from business acumen to fame and whether a person is going to travel long distances.

Although fortune-tellers swear that their readings are accurate, fortune-telling is classed by many as a pseudoscience, lacking any scientific evidentiary substance.

How Intelligent Are Dolphins?

Dolphins are generally considered to be the most intelligent animal in the entire animal kingdom, and the bottlenose dolphin is thought to be the smartest species of the bunch.

Dolphins are gregarious and social by nature, which is indicative of intelligence. They live in pods and communicate via an intricate array of clicks and whistles, also using ultrasonic sonar to communicate and locate food. They are capable of forming strong bonds with each other.

Dolphins are often comfortable in the presence of humans and have been known to protect humans from shark attacks.

They have a high capacity for learning and are capable of extraordinary acrobatic feats in the water. It is thought that they do this in a playful manner, although they can be quickly trained by humans to perform for audiences. Dolphins have also been used in working with disabled children, while military organizations have put them to work in finding mines and helping rescue operations. They have also been known to guide boats through treacherous reefs.

The size of an animal's brain is often an indication of intelligence. The dolphin's brain is large; in fact, its frontal lobe—the area of the brain thought to relate particularly to intelligence—is larger than that of a human. Their brains also have a highly structured cortex. Dolphins are capable of recognizing sign language used by humans and can recognize themselves in a mirror, showing a level of self-awareness that is very rare in animals and is considered to be a trait of intelligence.

While the testing of the intelligence of dolphins is continuing, it is limited by its expense and the inherent difficulties involved in the testing process.

Can a Person Be Frozen and Then Brought Back to Life?

Science fiction films often portray people who have been frozen and then restored to life. Although this scenario is considered by many to be fanciful, with advances in modern technology, it just might become possible.

Cryonics is the preservation of bodies at extremely low temperatures. Although bacteria and even small animals, such as frogs, can be frozen and then returned to a living state when thawed, larger animals, such as humans, cannot. This is because the freezing process of removing heat through thick tissue is too slow, and ice crystals grow and damage the body's cells irreparably. But using cryoprotectants, which allow water to vitrify rather than freeze, prevents ice crystals from forming. Vitrification does not freeze tissue but preserves it in a glassy state. This prevents the molecules from rearranging themselves.

Some scientists believe a body vitrified using cryoprotectants could remain physically viable for thirty thousand years without damage to the structure of the brain. Although today's technology does not allow a frozen person to be revived, some believe that in the future—as medical technology improves—it could become a reality.

Although the practice is viewed with skepticism by most medical professionals, some scientists ardently believe in it. Cryonicists claim that even though a person is dead, if they are vitrified immediately after death, their organs could remain viable, just as a heart to be transplanted comes from a person who is dead but whose heart still beats.

A number of people have undergone this process in the hope that future technology will allow them to be revived, but the procedure and continued storage of the body are far too expensive for most people to afford. Only time will tell if the expense is worth it.

Why Were Neckties Invented?

It is often questioned why such a seemingly useless item of apparel as the necktie was ever invented. It's thought by some anthropologists that it might have been the first item of clothing ever worn, taking the form of a strip of fur around the necks of our ancestors. However, the earliest evidence of the wearing of neckties was by the Chinese. China's first emperor, Shih Huang Ti, was afraid of death and commanded that replicas of his army personnel be laid to rest with him for protection. He died in 210 BC, and when his tomb was rediscovered in 1974, the intricately detailed terracotta replicas preserved therein each wore neck cloths or ties.

Neckties were also present in Roman times. In AD 113, after one of his victories, the emperor Trajan erected a marble column bearing reliefs that feature thousands of soldiers, many of whom are wearing neckties. It's thought by some that these soldiers wore neckties to guard against cold weather or to absorb sweat.

While neckties have been around in one form or another for millennia, it was because of the Croatians in the 17th century that wearing them became a statement of fashion. After helping in a victory against the Habsburg Empire, thousands of soldiers were presented to King Louis XIV in Paris, among them a regiment of Croatian marines, some of whom wore colorful cravats. These embellishments appealed to the French, who had never seen such an article of clothing and who were soon wearing similar cravats. Until the French Revolution in 1789, the French maintained an elite regiment known as the *Cravate Royale*, and the word "cravat" itself is from the French word *cravate*, meaning "Croatian."

It wasn't long before the wearing of neckties spread. In 1660, Charles II returned to England from exile and reclaimed the throne that he had lost during the English Civil War. He was followed by aristocrats who brought the cravat to England, whereupon it developed into the necktie, became popular, and spread throughout Europe, then the US and then the rest of the world.

Is Jurassic Park Possible?

In the 1993 movie *Jurassic Park*, dinosaurs are cloned from DNA found in mosquitoes that have been preserved for millions of years. The dinosaur DNA is spliced with frog DNA to make it complete and placed in ostrich eggs, out of which hatch dinosaurs. There are many compelling reasons why this process could not work and why the cloning of dinosaurs is not possible.

The dinosaur DNA would be mixed with mosquito DNA, which might contain DNA from a number of species of dinosaur, meaning replication of a single species would not be possible. In any event, enzymes in the mosquitoes would break down the dinosaur DNA, so the mosquitoes would need to be preserved immediately after feeding on dinosaur blood.

Although dinosaur DNA has been found in real life, it is always broken apart and needs to be sequenced. This cannot be done because there are no complete strands of dinosaur DNA available to copy. Even if it could be properly sequenced, dinosaur DNA would have gaps. Every chromosome must be present, and this is never the case with DNA that has been preserved for millions of years. The fossilization process alters molecules in the DNA. These gaps in the dinosaur DNA cannot be filled by splicing dinosaur DNA with frog DNA, as this process would not produce a dinosaur. And even if sequenced and complete dinosaur DNA were available, it would need to be inserted into an oocyte (a female germ cell, which gives rise to an ovum) from a dinosaur. As no dinosaurs now exist, there are no dinosaur oocytes. If all of these factors were present, a dinosaur egg would be needed from which to hatch the dinosaur. Only a dinosaur egg could provide the hormones and other nutrients to nourish a developing dinosaur.

These numerous factors mean that with today's technology, cloning dinosaurs is impossible.

How Do Squirrels Find Their Buried Nuts?

Squirrels are often seen either hiding nuts or digging them up to eat. They bury nuts so that they have food during the lean winter months. With the nuts so small and the areas in which they are buried so large, people sometimes question just how the squirrels find the nuts when they need them.

Scientists believe that squirrels possess an excellent spatial memory and make a mental map of where they bury their nuts. They also remember particular landmarks and different aspects of the environment to help them find the nuts.

The squirrel uses another cunning technique to find nuts. Before burying them, the squirrel will break the shell of the nut with its teeth and then clean the nut by rubbing it on its face or licking it. This applies the squirrel's scent to the nut. Using its acute sense of smell, the squirrel is then able to locate the nut, even when it is covered by thick snow.

Of course, many nuts are never found, and this provides a good source of future trees.

Why Is the Color Yellow Associated with Cowards?

The color yellow has traditionally been associated with cowards. Even today, cowards are sometimes called yellow.

Yellow has had this connotation since the 1800s. The term "yellow dog" was used to describe cowardly people at that time, and the term "yellow belly" was used in American slang in the early 20th century to describe a person who lacked courage.

It is not entirely clear why yellow was used to refer to cowards.

The color yellow (although not the term) has been associated with treachery and cowardice for centuries. In France, the doors of traitors were painted yellow. Paintings of Judas, the Apostle who betrayed Jesus, show him wearing yellow robes. Additionally, victims of the Spanish Inquisition wore yellow. A yellow flag was a symbol of quarantine for victims of yellow fever, and the term "yellow journalism" (which employed sensational headlines) dates to the 1800s.

Although any of these could be the origin of the color's association with cowardice, a more compelling theory is from a principle of medicine dating back to the Middle Ages that there are four humors, or fluids, in the body, which determine a person's physical and mental health. It was thought that if any of the humors became imbalanced, ill health would result. The four humors are blood, phlegm, black bile, and yellow bile, and it is yellow bile that makes a person irritable, choleric, and liable to act irrationally.

Why Do Some People Wear High Heels?

A high-heeled shoe is one that raises the heel of the foot significantly higher than the toes. (When both the heel and the toes are raised, the shoe is called a platform shoe.) Women have worn high-heeled shoes for centuries, typically on formal occasions. Paintings from ancient Egypt depict women wearing high-heeled shoes as far back as 4000 BC.

A woman wears high heels to seem taller and change her posture. They make the calves appear more defined, as well as emphasize the femininity of a woman's walk by causing the buttocks to protrude and sway.

But high heels are often uncomfortable to wear, are difficult to walk in, and can cause damage to a woman's feet, ankles, and tendons. This means that many women have a love-hate relationship with high-heeled shoes.

What Are the Origins of the Expressions "On the Wagon" and "One for the Road"?

The phrase "on the wagon" refers to refraining from drinking alcohol for a time; "one for the road" refers to one last drink before leaving, which will make the ride home more enjoyable.

One theory is that "on the wagon" derives from the water wagons in America's past before the roads were paved. In order to keep down dust, horse-drawn water wagons would spray the streets. Anyone who had sworn off alcohol was said to have "climbed aboard the water wagon." Although this may be the origin of the phrase, there is another more colorful explanation, which relates to "one for the road" as well.

It is thought that in London in the days of public hangings, the condemned man would be taken through the town to the gallows on a wagon. Some say he was allowed one drink at every tavern on the way, so that he was drunk by the time he reached his place of death. At the last pub, he was given "one for the road" before he was put "on the wagon," never to drink again. Another theory is that he would be given only one drink along the way, while still another is that the driver would have "one for the road" while the prisoner, who was not allowed to drink, was "on the wagon." Others believe it was the prisoner who had "one for the road," while the driver was left "on the wagon."

Why Do Geese Fly in a V Formation?

When a flock of geese migrate, they generally fly in a V formation. Until recently, scientists could only guess why geese did this, but it is now known that there are a number of logical reasons for the behavior.

Many ornithologists believed that this form of flying conserves energy, but there was no physical evidence of this. Then a team of scientists attached heart monitors to a flock of birds. When flying in a V formation, it was found that the heart rates of the birds are much lower than when they fly solo. Flying in a V formation reduces the wind resistance for some of the birds and allows them to glide and conserve energy. This is because the lead birds break the air and create an uplifting draft. Similar to a team of cyclists, the lead birds regularly swap positions to recover, allowing other birds to take their place. Indeed, it has been shown that birds can fly 70 percent farther when in a V formation than when alone.

Scientists also believe that geese fly in this way so that it is easier to see and keep track of the entire flock and to allow the geese to communicate during their long flights. Fighter pilots also use this technique to better see each other. In addition, because of where the eyes of the goose are situated on the sides of the head, if geese flew exactly behind each other, they would need to tilt their heads to the side to properly see the other geese. This would result in asymmetrical wing movements, which would not be as aerodynamic or as energy efficient.

Why Do People Often Wake Up Just before the Alarm?

Some people find that, no matter what time they go to bed, they wake at the same time every morning, quite often just before their alarm clock sounds.

Scientists believe that a person wakes at the same time each day because of the body's circadian rhythms, the internal "body clock" that regulates the cyclic processes of the body over a twenty-four-hour period. These rhythms are important in determining the sleep patterns of people and are thought to be predominantly internal (that is, not affected by external stimuli), being affected and largely defined by regular activity in people, which goes some way to explaining why people generally wake up at around the same time every day. Studies have also shown that a person's body temperature rises at the same time each morning, which is also linked to waking.

Waking just before the alarm is thought to be the work of the subconscious. People anticipate the time they're going to wake up, and this anticipation makes them wake just before the alarm goes off. Both waking and the sound of the alarm cause stress, so the subconscious sets a time of waking just before the alarm goes off. The theory is that, if people think of an exact time they are going to awaken and imagine themselves waking at that time, the subconscious takes over while they're asleep and makes this happen. Indeed, some studies have shown an increase in certain hormones in the body that wake a person in circumstances when they were aware of the time that the alarm was due to go off, caused by the subconscious anticipating this time and prompting the body to wake itself.

Why Does Spicy Food Make the Eyes and Nose Water?

A common symptom of eating spicy food is watering of the eyes and nose. This is caused by two different chemicals, depending on the type of food eaten.

When it comes to chili peppers, it's capsaicin. Capsaicin is an alkaloid substance contained primarily in the membrane of the pepper that the seeds attach to. Capsaicin exists to deter mammals from eating the fruit. It stimulates nerve receptors in the tongue that sense heat and pain, causing a burning sensation. It is also a key ingredient in pepper spray.

Allyl isothiocyanate is a colorless oil found in mustard, horseradish, wasabi, and radishes. Like capsaicin, it acts as a defensive mechanism against mammals. It is also used as an ingredient in insecticides and fungicides.

Both capsaicin and allyl isothiocyanate cause a burning sensation on your tongue, and they also irritate the mucous membranes in your nose. The membranes become inflamed, which triggers them to produce extra mucus. This is a defense mechanism against the unwanted substance causing the irritation, preventing it from entering your respiratory system. The membranes in your eyes also get irritated by these chemicals, causing your tear ducts to produce more fluid in an attempt to wash the irritant away. The more irritated your nose and eyes become, the more liquid they produce in defense.

Various tissues in your body, such as your intestines, are also irritated by capsaicin and allyl isothiocyanate. The irritation causes the body to try to flush them out, which sometimes results in diarrhea.

The best way to nullify these symptoms is by drinking milk. Both chemicals have an oily quality that renders water ineffective. Milk, however, contains the protein casein, which is a lipophilic molecule that binds to the heat-forming molecules and washes them away. Eating sugar can also produce a chemical reaction that reduces the heat.

❓ Did the Lost City of Atlantis Exist?

The lost city of Atlantis is fabled as a utopian city that was destroyed in ancient times. The Greek philosopher Plato described it in 360 BC as a city of wealth and natural beauty, with an advanced civilization. He said that it flourished for nine thousand years before being destroyed by an earthquake and a tidal wave. Scholars have searched for it for centuries, with much debate as to where it might have been, if anywhere. It has been placed near Cuba; Devon, England; Antarctica; and Indonesia. Some place it in the middle of the Atlantic Ocean.

Many believed it to be merely a mythical island, but Plato claimed it was somewhere west of the Pillars of Hercules, which are at one end of the Strait of Gibraltar. The only accounts of the city are in Plato's *Timaeus and Critias*, where he says that, "In a single day and night of misfortune, the City of Atlantis fell into the sea."

Interest in Atlantis began in earnest in 1882, when books were written about it. This interest continued to modern times, and in 1938, leading member of the German Nazi Party Heinrich Himmler organized a search for it. No conclusive evidence was found for the existence of the city, with many believing that Plato's story was derived from mythology.

However, fairly recent research reported by an archaeology journal called *Antiquity* claims that Atlantis might lie in a salt marsh region off Spain's southern coast, near the port of Cadiz. Ancient ruins that appear on satellite images conform to Plato's city. Two rectangular buildings surrounded by concentric circles can be seen, and these accord with what Plato described. Plato also claimed that the diameter of the largest circle was 5 kilometers (3.1 miles), and the satellite images show that it is in fact between 5 and 6 kilometers (3.1 and 3.7 miles). Some experts now believe that thousands of years ago, rising waters may well have submerged the city, not in one day as Plato suggests, but over hundreds of years. More research will still have to be done to convince the many skeptics, but it seems that the lost city may have existed after all.

Why Was 911 Chosen as the Emergency Number?

The best-known phone number in the world is probably 911. It is the emergency number throughout the United States and is known in many other countries that broadcast the television show *Rescue 911*. But were those numbers just picked at random, or was there some logic to them?

Before the 1960s, the United States didn't have a universal emergency phone number. People had to call different numbers for each emergency department in their local area. This made things very confusing. With thousands of numbers being used across America, each household had to know lengthy numbers for reaching firefighters, police, or ambulances.

Then in 1957, the National Association of Fire Chiefs recommended the use of a single phone number for reporting fires. But it wasn't until 1967 that various government agencies supported this idea and directed the Federal Communications Commission to come up with a solution.

After discussions between the FCC and AT&T, it was announced in 1968 that the emergency number would be 911. But why 911?

The number was chosen for a variety of reasons. Most importantly, it was short and could be dialed quickly using the old-style rotary phones, which still existed at the time. And being so brief, it was easy to remember. Another key factor was that it was unique and had never been used as a code in America before—not an office code, an area code, or a service code.

It could also be easily distinguished from other, longer phone numbers in AT&T's internal system, which meant it could be routed to a special location with minimal changes to the AT&T network.

The first 911 call was made on February 16, 1968, by Senator Rankin Fite in Haleyville, Alabama. Now, an estimated 240 million calls are made to the number each year in the United States.

Why Do Girls Throw Like a Girl?

As a schoolboy, there is no more embarrassing taunt than being told that you throw like a girl. There are a lot of other disparaging ways that boys can be likened to girls, but what makes the throwing jibe so offensive?

It's because the "throwing gap," as it is known, is the biggest difference between the genders. Janet Hyde, a professor of psychology and women's studies at the University of Wisconsin, has studied the gender gap in detail across a number of areas, ranging from behavioral, psychological, communication, and physical. She found that men and women are very alike, far more than people believe, in all areas except for one: throwing. Based on standard deviations from the mean, she measured a variety of differences, including physical aggression (which was 0.60 standard deviations in favor of men—not high significance), and grip strength (which was 0.66 toward men—not high significance). But when it came to throwing velocity and throwing distance, the figures skewed markedly, and were well above anything else, both physical and psychological. Throwing speed was 2.18 standard deviations in favor of men, and distance was 1.98 in favor of men.

So, how do girls throw? Girls take a small step on the same side as the hand they throw with, propelling their forearm in a weak motion, which actually negates forward thrust. Boys, on the other hand, use their whole body, stepping forward with the opposite foot, rotating with the hips and shoulders, and whipping with the arm and hand. This rotation is the key to power in a throw. While girls tend to rotate their shoulders and hips together, in boys the hips rotate forward independently, before the shoulders snap around. This results in a far more powerful throw for boys.

Some claim that boys are better at throwing because they've practiced more from a young age or because of their superior strength, but in most societies, this does not seem to be the case. Before puberty, the physical differences between boys and girls are not enough to account for the throwing gap, and even at the age of four, the gap is three times greater than any other motor function. By age fifteen, nearly every boy throws better than the best girl does.

But what is the explanation for the throwing gap? Once again, it's evolution. Our early ancestors survived by hunting, and the most important trait for hunting was throwing, be it a spear or a rock. The man with the most powerful and accurate throw killed the most animals to feed his family, and his genes were more likely to be passed down. Women, on the other hand, did not hunt, so had no reason to develop good throwing skills.

What Happens When a Person Is in a Coma?

A coma is a state of unconsciousness. The word comes from the Greek word *koma* meaning "deep sleep." A coma patient is alive but is usually unable to move or respond. As a coma deepens, the brain becomes less responsive to pain or any other factor, and it becomes less likely that the patient will come out of it.

Comas are to be distinguished from brain death, when all brain activity ceases. A brain-dead person is unable to breathe, whereas a coma patient often can. A coma is also different from a state of vegetation, which may follow a coma. In a vegetative state, a person has usually lost environmental awareness but still has noncognitive functioning. Schizophrenia and catatonia can sometimes result in comatose-like behavior, but these, too, are different conditions.

A coma can result from a variety of causes. Central nervous system diseases and drug and alcohol intoxication are common causes. Diffuse pathologies are responsible for around 60 percent of cases. These include head trauma and intoxication. Expanding lesions and vascular problems can also result in a coma.

Comas typically last a few weeks, and people usually "wake up" progressively over a number of days. Whether a person comes out of a coma depends on the severity of the damage to the brain, and people who come out often exhibit physical, psychological, or intellectual problems. Recovery is usually gradual.

Debate rages as to whether coma patients should be kept alive for extended periods on life support.

Can Ouija Boards Be Used to Contact Spirits?

A Ouija board is a device that people use to communicate with spirits during a séance. The board is covered with numbers, figures, and symbols. Participants place their fingers on a small wooden or plastic tablet called a planchette, which then, according to adherents, moves around the board to spell out messages from spirits.

Many superstitions surround the use of Ouija boards and séances, but believers say that as long as a number of rules are followed, such as never playing alone, no harm can result. Other proponents think Ouija boards are a dangerous tool that should not be taken lightly because of the ability of inexperienced users to contact harmful spirits and demons.

Some people have reported seeing ghosts and hearing voices during séances.

Skeptics do not believe that Ouija boards can contact spirits. Most psychologists think that participants make small, involuntary movements unconsciously and attribute them to paranormal forces. This is known as the ideomotor effect. It can be very powerful, and people might find it impossible to be convinced that it is in fact their subconscious that is making their own hands move. Psychologists say that people often want to believe in the unlikely and are willing to trick themselves to this end. Other skeptics claim that the movements are caused by a manipulative participant who is trying to fool the other players. No scientific evidence has ever been presented to support the successful use of Ouija boards.

Ouija board is a trademark, although people often make boards by hand and use an overturned glass or a coin as the planchette.

Why Do Onions Make People Cry?

It's not the strong odor of onions that makes us cry when we cut them, but the gas that they emit, which is also responsible for their pungent taste and for the bad breath they can cause.

Onions contain a sulfur-based oil. When cut, the cells that contain the sulphur compounds are broken and the compounds are converted into sulfenic acid, which in turn produces a highly volatile chemical called syn-Propanethial-S-oxide, which then rises into the air. When this chemical comes into contact with our eyes, it reacts with the moisture in our eyelids and results in the production of sulfuric acid, which irritates the eyes and stimulates the lacrimal glands. When stimulated, these glands release tears to flush out the acid and protect the eye. Rubbing the eyes with the hands can often exacerbate the problem, especially if the hands are covered with oil from the onion.

There are a variety of ways of preventing the gases emitted by the onion from reaching the eyes. Moving your head away from the onion so that the gas disperses is one such method, while another is to cook the onion first, or even cool it in the fridge; both methods serve to change the compounds in the onion. Breathing with an open mouth can also help, as it means you'll suck away some of the gases before they reach your eyes. Probably the best and easiest method, however, is to cut the onion under running water, which washes away the gases before they can reach the eyes.

Why Are Airplane Cabin Lights Dimmed for Takeoff and Landing?

How many times does it happen? You're on a plane and in the middle of reading a key part of your book when an announcement is made that the plane is preparing to land, and the cabin lights are about to be dimmed. You have to resort to that tiny light above your head, which frankly does nothing and shouldn't even be called a light. The pilot never explains the reason for this dimming, at most just saying it is protocol for nighttime landings. Why do they do it?

The dimming of the lights during takeoff and landing could be the difference between life and death. Those times are considered the most critical and are when most accidents happen, so the lights are dimmed as a standard safety measure.

The purpose of dimming the lights is to match the cabin environment to the exterior environment. This is done to prepare for a potential evacuation in the dark. Going from a brightly lit cabin into the outside darkness would require a period of visual adjustment that could cost precious seconds. But with the lights already dimmed, the passengers' eyes would already be accustomed to the outside conditions, and this would facilitate a safer and faster escape. For example, with the eyes already adjusted, a passenger would be able to locate an exit or an evacuation slide more quickly.

This is also the reason why cabin window shades are raised. It assists with adjusting the passengers' eyes to the outside light, as well.

This is what all the airlines claim, anyway. The real reason is they just don't want you to finish your book.

What Is Truth Serum and Does It Work?

Truth serum is a drug used to try to obtain accurate answers from a person who is being questioned. It is normally used by police or military interrogators. Its existence has been popularized by many motion pictures, including the James Bond film *Octopussy*, Arnold Schwarzenegger's *True Lies*, and Quentin Tarantino's *Kill Bill*.

A number of sedatives have been used as truth serums, but the most common is sodium thiopental, also known as sodium pentothal. This yellow crystal can be dissolved in alcohol or water.

Sodium pentothal interferes with the part of the brain that controls judgment. Patients typically lose their normal inhibitions and become very communicative. The drug slows the central nervous system, reducing the heart rate and blood pressure. It minimizes stress and excitement and makes patients more relaxed and open to suggestion. This might make patients more likely to tell the truth.

But although patients' inhibitions are lowered, they do not lose self-control and so are still able to lie, fantasize, or be manipulated into telling lies.

Truth serums were tested in the United States in the 1950s, and although they can be effective facilitators of questioning, they were found not to be the magical drug that some had claimed. In fact, studies show that information obtained through truth serums is often unreliable, and although some assert that government agencies possess more powerful and successful truth drugs, anesthetics experts doubt this claim.

A number of US court decisions have disallowed evidence obtained using truth serum, finding such testimony unreliable.

Why Did Dinosaurs Become Extinct?

The dinosaurs became extinct about 65 million years ago, having existed for more than 165 million years. Their time on Earth amounts to around 75 percent of the history of the planet, making their extensive dominance the most successful of nearly any life-form. The reason such a flourishing group went extinct has been the subject of much research, and until recently was one of the most perplexing riddles facing paleontologists.

Despite years of research, it is only since 1980 that scientists have had some firm evidence about the cause of the demise of the dinosaurs. A theory was proposed by geologist Walter

Alvarez, whose team discovered fossilized sedimentary layers across the world from the end of the Cretaceous Period and the start of the Paleogene Period, 65 million years ago (known as the Cretaceous-Paleogene boundary). The fossils contain a high concentration of iridium, an element that is rare on Earth but common in objects such as asteroids and comets. Alvarez concluded that a 10-kilometer-wide asteroid collided with Earth and led to the death of the dinosaurs. It is known as the K-Pg extinction event (K being an abbreviation of Cretaceous). Evidence has now been found that such an asteroid did slam into Yucatán.

A collision of that magnitude would have been millions of times more powerful than any nuclear weapon and would have resulted in enormous hurricanes and a worldwide firestorm. Dust from extensive storms would have filled the atmosphere, blocking sunlight for years, producing acid rain, and dramatically reducing world temperatures, thus wiping out the dinosaurs.

Although most scientists agree that the K-Pg event led to the extinction of the dinosaurs, it is unknown whether they died off rapidly. The majority of experts favor this view. But another theory is that increased volcanic activity across the world made oxygen decrease and temperatures drop, killing off the dinosaurs gradually. Some say that the dinosaurs were killed by disease as they migrated throughout the world, but most experts think that this is unlikely.

Why Are Children's Coin Banks Called Piggy Banks?

A piggy bank is a traditional container, used mainly by children, in which to store coins. Piggy banks are often shaped like pigs, yet, contrary to popular belief, the name is not derived from "pig."

Although the exact origin of the piggy bank is not clear, historians believe that it was first used in the Middle Ages in England. In the 1500s, people often kept coins in "pygg jars." Metal was expensive, and pygg was a cheap clay used for making household objects, such as jars and pots.

By the 1700s, pygg was pronounced "pig," and it is likely that potters who received requests to make pygg jars or banks mistakenly made them in the shape of a pig.

The comically shaped coin banks appealed to children, and they are still popular today.

Don't Police Sirens Alert the Bad Guys That the Cops Are on Their Way?

Picture the scene: You've got the balaclava on, the customers are lying on the ground, you've controlled the bank staff well, their hands are in the air, and you're sure nobody's hit the panic button. Most of the money is in the bags, but you've got all the time in the world, so you keep stuffing more of it in there. Suddenly, you hear the sirens. No! Someone must have called the cops. Luckily, you can hear the sirens in the distance, so there's now time to escape. If they hadn't put those sirens on, you could have been in all sorts of trouble. Why on earth did they give the game away like that?

The main reason why police use their sirens is to get to the scene safely and without harm to others. A siren alerts other motorists and tells them to make way for a fast-moving vehicle. It also warns pedestrians to keep clear. In addition, a police car does not technically become an emergency vehicle until both its lights and siren are activated. Until that time, the officer is bound by all applicable traffic rules and can't lawfully violate stop signs and red lights. If a crash occurs while the lights and sirens are on, the officer's liability is far more likely to be reduced.

But whether the siren is sounded or not often depends on the situation. For example:

- In most robberies, the suspect has already gone by the time the police are notified, so the siren helps them get to the scene faster.
- Alerting the suspect by using the siren can assist police, as the siren can prompt a fleeing suspect to hide as opposed to running. This can give the police a chance to establish a perimeter and trap a suspect, later flushing the suspect out with dogs.
- If a violent assault is in progress, the use of the siren may cause the assailant to break off the attack and flee earlier than they would have otherwise. In many cases, this could save a victim's life.

- Hearing the siren may decrease an attacker's morale while increasing the confidence of any police at the scene, giving the police an edge.
- In cases where a burglary is in process, and it's unlikely anyone will be injured, the police often turn their sirens off a few minutes before arriving in the hope of retaining the element of surprise and apprehending the suspect.

In the end, it depends on the circumstances, and the use of the siren is all a matter of balancing the safety considerations with the tactical benefits.

How Do Spiders Spin Webs, and Why Don't They Get Stuck in Them?

A spider has two parts to its body, one of which produces silk. The silk is produced in glands in the abdomen and passed through tiny holes at the tip of the abdomen, which compress the silk. The silk starts in liquid form but immediately becomes solid when exposed to air.

A spider uses different glands to produce different types of silk. Sticky silk is designed to catch insects while a stronger, nonstick silk is used to tie down the web and to serve as its frame. Still a different type of silk is used to build its cocoons. Some of the strands in a spiderweb are stronger than strands of steel of the same thickness.

Spiderwebs begin with a single thread, which is usually cast into the wind from a high vantage point. If the thread catches on to another branch, for example, the spider then walks along it, releases a looser thread below the first one, and lays a number of anchor points. From there, the spider is able to spin its web.

The spider uses its nonstick silk to make the frame of its web and the threads that run out from the center. This is because the spider needs to walk along the structure to weave the rest of the web and to traverse the web generally. A spider also has legs that are covered in an oily coating that helps to prevent it from getting stuck in its own web. But, if a spider is startled and falls onto the sticky silk of its web, it is possible for the spider to become entangled in its own web.

Why Is a Person's Signature Called Their "John Hancock"?

John Hancock was an American merchant and diplomat who lived from 1737 to 1793. He was the governor of Massachusetts and president of the Second Continental Congress. He's known to more people now than he was almost 300 years ago, in large part because his name has become synonymous with any signature. "Just put your John Hancock here and the deal will be done." Why do people say things like that?

Because John Hancock had a massive signature, and he was proud of it.

Hancock was one of the men to sign the American Declaration of Independence in 1776. His flamboyant signature is by far the largest on the document, measuring nearly five inches long. It is told that when he signed the document, he said with a laugh, "There—I guess King George or John Bull will be able to read that without his spectacles."

And that's why your signature today is called your John Hancock.

❓ Do Sharks Have to Keep Swimming to Stay Alive?

Take a visit to any large aquarium that has sharks, and you're sure to hear people saying with confidence that sharks have to keep swimming to stay alive, and if they stop, they'll die. Is there any truth to this?

Like other fish, sharks breathe through their gills, which are respiratory organs equivalent to our lungs. As water passes over the gill membranes, blood vessels extract oxygen from the water. How the sharks force the water over their gills differs among the species.

Most sharks (about 94 percent of the 400 species) can stay alive without constantly swimming. These older species physically filter water over their gills using their cheek muscles. This is known as buccal pumping. These sharks, which include the nurse and bullhead sharks, can alternate between swimming and rest.

As sharks evolved and became more active, this method of pumping water became secondary, and it was more efficient simply to take in water while swimming. This method of

breathing is known as ram ventilation—the shark "rams" water into its open mouth while it swims, and the water flows over its gills.

While some sharks, such as the sand tiger shark, can alternate between these two techniques, about two dozen species rely solely on ram ventilation. They have lost the buccal pumping anatomy, so they must keep swimming in order to stay alive. Apart from stopping briefly from time to time, these sharks would die from a lack of oxygen if they stopped swimming for a longer period.

Sharks that must constantly swim include the great white, the whale shark, and the mako shark. Don't feel too sorry for them, though; it's actually less work for these sharks to swim than to remain still.

When Was Toilet Paper Invented, and What Was Used before Then?

The Chinese invented toilet paper in the 14th century, and the Bureau of Imperial Supplies began to produce paper for use by the Chinese emperors. However, it wasn't until 1857 that the first factory-produced toilet paper was made, by American Joseph Gayetty, who named his product "Therapeutic Paper" and sold it in packs of 500 sheets. Gayetty's name was printed on each sheet.

Before the invention of toilet paper, different areas of the world used many different things. Public toilets in ancient Rome provided a moist sponge on the end of a stick, while the wealthy used wool and rosewater. In Viking-occupied England, discarded wool was used, while in the Middle Ages this had been replaced by hay balls.

In Hawaii, meanwhile, coconut husks were used, while the early Eskimos used snow and tundra moss. Wealthy people around the world often used hemp and wool, with lace being used by the French royalty. British lords used pages from books.

Poorer people used their hands, grass, stones, moss, seashells, or wood shavings, while the use of water was also common around the world. In India, the left hand was used to wash with, while in Africa it was the right hand. The other hand in each place was used to greet people, and it was considered rude to offer the incorrect hand.

In the US, newspapers and telephone directories were commonly used, as were other books. *The Old Farmer's Almanac* was actually printed with a hole punched through the corner of each page so that it could be hung in outhouses, and the Sears catalog was widely used until it was produced with glossy pages, after which its use as a hygiene product became unpopular. Corncobs were also used in the United States.

💡 Why Does Bacon Smell So Good?

Very few aromas will get a person's mouth watering like the smell of bacon cooking. Even vegetarians have been known to falter under its powers. But what makes it different from other meats?

When bacon is cooked, it undergoes a process called the Maillard reaction. Named after the 20th-century French chemist Louis-Camille Maillard, the Maillard reaction is the chemical process responsible for turning food brown and giving it aroma and flavor. When bacon is heated, the molecular structure of its sugars begins to break down and react with the amino acids that are released. For bacon, this reaction releases about 150 complex aroma compounds, far more than for other foods.

The majority of these compounds are hydrocarbons and aldehydes, both of which give off delicious smells. This happens with most meats, but bacon has a secret weapon. When bacon has been cured with salt or brine, it contains a higher percentage of nitrates, specifically pyridines, than other meats have. When pyridines mix with the hydrocarbons and aldehydes, a volatile combination explodes, and that's what gives bacon its unique smell.

Why Do Vultures Circle Above Their Prey?

Vultures are a common sight in the skies above the American and African plains. These scavenging birds of prey are often seen circling in the sky before flying down and eating a meal. This has led people to question why they waste their time circling above, instead of going straight down to eat. There are a number of reasons for this behavior.

Contrary to popular belief, circling vultures do not necessarily indicate there is a dead animal below. They soar on warm, rising thermal wind currents for various reasons—to conserve energy, to gain altitude for long flights, and to search for food.

When they are looking for food, vultures locate it by using both sight and smell. By flying high up and circling the ground, they are able to scan a large area for food with their excellent vision. They also have a keen sense of smell, and circling may indicate that they have detected a carcass and are trying to pinpoint its exact location.

Once the vultures have located food, they will often swoop straight down and eat it. But when they keep circling, it is likely to be for one of the following reasons:

- While vultures usually feed on carrion, they will sometimes kill injured or helpless animals. They are, however, very cautious about approaching a live animal, and may circle to ensure it is really dead or incapacitated and therefore not a threat.
- Vultures will always check for any predators that might be in the area, such as a coyote or lion. To scan the area for dangerous animals, they will circle before descending to their meal.
- Vultures will circle over a kill made by a larger predator, like a lion. Lions won't share their kill and will attack any vultures that venture too close. While they're biding their time and waiting for their chance, they will often remain in the safety of the sky.
- If they see a lot of animal activity below, they will sometimes circle around waiting for a predator to make a kill that they might be able to scavenge.

So, there are a number of valid reasons for vultures to circle the sky, or maybe they're just having fun.

How and Why Do Chameleon Lizards Change Color?

The chameleon is a small lizard, found mainly in Africa and Madagascar (but also parts of Europe and Asia), that is famous for being able to change its color.

Most people believe that the chameleon changes color as a means of camouflage—it blends in with its surroundings. Not true. The lizard changes color depending on its physical or emotional disposition at the time. Chameleons change color in response to changes in light and temperature. The change of colors also depends on the mood of the lizard and plays a major role in its communication with other chameleons. Possible colors range from brown and green to red, blue, and yellow. Coincidentally, brown and green often match the chameleon's background, which leads people to think that camouflage is the reason for a change.

In cold conditions, a chameleon will turn a darker color to absorb more heat, and in hot and bright conditions, a chameleon will turn a lighter color to reflect the heat. To attract a mate, a male chameleon will exhibit his brightest and most impressive colors. If a rival male approaches, he will turn a bright color, such as red, indicating that he is a healthy specimen and ready to fight. If a chameleon is scared, it will often turn a dark color.

Chameleons are able to change colors because of their unusual genetics. Special cells lie in layers beneath their transparent skin. The upper layer contains red and yellow pigments, while the lower layer contains a colorless substance that reflects the blue part of light. Under these cells is a dark layer of melanin. This melanin influences how light or dark the reflected light is. Depending on the temperature, the brightness, or the chameleon's mood, hormones trigger the chameleon's brain to send a signal to activate particular cells. This message tells the cells to expand or contract, redistributing their colors and creating a different overall color for the lizard. For example, if the upper cells are yellow and the lower cells reflect the blue part of light, the colors mix and the chameleon appears green. The result of this unique chemistry is a lizard that can produce a wide variety of different colors to suit its circumstances.

❓ Does an Apple a Day Keep the Doctor Away?

Dating from the 1860s, "An apple a day keeps the doctor away" is one of our most recognizable expressions. But is there any medical truth to it?

Numerous studies have been conducted regarding apples and their health properties. The fruit undoubtedly has many benefits and, as a rule, more benefits than most other fruits.

Apples contain pectin, a form of soluble fiber that lowers blood pressure and glucose levels. They also contain boron, which is known to support strong bones and a healthy brain, as well as vitamin C, which boosts immunity and overall health. Studies have shown that eating apples lowers cholesterol, reduces the risk of strokes and diabetes, helps with allergies, and can help regulate a person's weight.

The peel of the apple provides the most health benefits. It contains phytonutrients, which are antioxidant compounds that fight potential damage from free radicals and significantly reduce the risk of heart disease, asthma, and cancer. In one Chinese clinical trial conducted between  2004 and 2014, apple eaters were shown to have a 40 percent lower chance of cardiovascular disease, a 34 percent lower chance of heart attack, and a 30 percent lower chance of stroke. Another study treated cancer cells with an extract from apple skin. Cancer cell growth was reduced by 43 to 57 percent, depending on the type of cancer.

Based on all of these findings, apples seem to be a superfood, but does eating one each day reduce visits to the doctor?

A 2015 study at the University of Michigan found that the people who ate an apple a day for a year did, in fact, visit the doctor fewer times during that year than those who didn't. However, these same people were less likely to smoke, tended to be more educated, and were less likely to be from an ethnic minority group. After adjusting for these differences, the researchers concluded that there was no statistical significance regarding apples and doctor visits.

So, an apple a day may not keep the doctor away, but, statistically speaking, it will reduce your chances of contracting major diseases and it will make you live longer. But the downside for kids is that you have to eat the skin for the real health benefits to kick in. Is there a trade-off? Apples act as a form of toothbrush, actually cleaning the teeth, so this might give kids an excuse not to brush. How do you like them apples?

Why Does Time Seem to Fly As We Get Older?

When we were children, summer vacation seemed to last forever. As we get older, it goes in the blink of an eye, prompting us to say comments like, "Where has the year gone?" and "Can you believe it's almost Christmas?" Why does our perception of time speed up with age?

It might make you feel a little better to know that this is a genuine phenomenon—time does seem to speed up. But it is not an exact science, so there are a number of competing theories.

1. **Biological clocks.** As we age, our metabolism slows, as do our heart rates and breathing. The slowing of these internal pacemakers, relative to the constant pace of real time, makes time seem to pass more quickly.

2. **Memorable events.** Another theory suggests that our perception of time is related to the number of memorable events we experience. This was first put forward by the American psychologist William James in his 1890 text *Principles of Psychology*. He believed that time speeds up as we age because it is accompanied by fewer and fewer memorable events. This lack of new experiences makes the days, weeks, and years smooth themselves out and pass in a blur. James went on to say that we might measure past intervals of time by the number of key events that can be recalled in that period. When we are young, numerous such events can take place in a short space of time (first kiss, learning to drive, graduation), making time seem to pass more slowly.

3. **New stimuli.** Similar to the memorable events theory, this hypothesis suggests that time is related to the amount of new information we receive. When faced with new situations, our brains record those memories in great detail. Everything is new when we are young, requiring us to use more brainpower to take it in. This makes time seem to pass more slowly. As we age, we become familiar with our surroundings and don't notice the details of our environments, making time run faster. It has been suggested

that the neurotransmitter dopamine is released when we see novel stimuli, and our levels of dopamine drop as we age, making time speed up.

4. **Attention.** As we age, we tend to pay less attention to time. Kids are always counting down the days until their birthday or a vacation, which can make the time seem to pass slowly. Meanwhile adults, who are busy working and dealing with life, don't focus on time as much. The next thing you know, a year has passed.

5. **Proportional theory.** The idea behind this theory is that time is measured on a logarithmic scale and that humans tend to perceive time proportionally to the length of time they have lived. This means for a four-year-old, one year is 25 percent of their lives, whereas to an 80-year-old, one year is just over 1 percent. This makes time seem to accelerate as we get older. On the logarithmic scale, a person would perceive the passage of time between ages one and two the same as they would perceive the passage of time between ages 10 and 20, or 20 and 40.

So, it turns out that the expression isn't quite right after all—time does fly. And, unfortunately, the older we get, the faster it flies.

Why Don't People Ride Zebras?

What's black and white and eats like a horse? A zebra. Zebras are very horse-like. They have manes and tails, eat grass, and are of a similar size and shape to horses. So, why don't we ride them?

Many people throughout history have attempted to tame, train, and ride zebras. The attempts proved both painstaking and dangerous. Most failed.

The main reason zebras can't be tamed is their aggressive disposition. Though domestic horses are known to kick and bite, zebras are different. When they kick, they look behind at their target, aiming and striking with power and purpose. They also lock on when they bite, holding on in an attempt to kill their foe. Zebras cause more injuries to zookeepers than any other animals do.

While the occasional single zebra has been partially tamed, it's proved impossible to domesticate herds. It is very difficult to lasso a zebra, as they watch the rope and duck their heads away at the last second. They are also bad-tempered, nervous, easily agitated, and run at the slightest provocation.

Given that zebras and horses share so many physical characteristics, why are horses so tolerant, but zebras aren't?

Evolution is the answer. While horses originated in the relatively safe environments of Asia and Europe, zebras evolved on the plains of Africa, sharing the space with many large predators such as lions, leopards, and crocodiles. Zebras are a prey species so, in order to survive, they developed intense early-warning mechanisms, making them extremely skittish. Their circumstances also made them more violent; when cornered or attacked, they were forced to fight for their lives.

Zebras also evolved alongside early humans, who used them as a food source. This means zebras inherently view people as a threat, and recent domestication attempts have not undone millennia of conditioning. Horses, on the other hand, evolved in the absence of early human, so they do not see us as such a threat.

It is because of these evolutionary factors that you won't see people competing on zebras in equestrian events for a long time to come.

Can the Full Moon Affect Human Behavior?

Since the Middle Ages, it has been said that the full moon has bizarre effects on human behavior. It is commonly thought to bring out the worst in people, increasing crime and suicide rates, making people more aggressive, and making accidents more prevalent. The influence of the full moon is known as the lunar effect. Even the word "lunacy" (meaning "insanity") is derived from the Latin word *lunar*, meaning "of or relating to the moon." In the 1800s, a murderer could rely on the defense of lunacy if the crime was committed during a full moon.

Even today, many people take the notion of a lunar effect seriously. Some studies in the United Kingdom show that car accidents rise by up to 50 percent during a full moon. A University of Miami psychologist, Arnold Lieber, also studied the homicide rate in Dade County for 15 years. He found an increased rate corresponded with the full moon throughout that time. He then repeated the experiment using data from Cleveland, Ohio, and the same result was found.

One proposed reason for the lunar effect is the perceived effect of the moon on the water contained in our bodies. Like the surface of Earth, the human body is 80 percent water. Some theorize that people experience some sort of biological tide, similar to the tides of the ocean.

Skeptics counter this argument by pointing out that, unlike the ocean, the amount of water in the body is far too small to have tides. Even landlocked lakes do not experience tides. In any event, the tides in oceans occur twice a day, not once a month, and the tidal force of the moon depends on the moon's distance from Earth and not on its phase. Skeptics also say that the full moons in the car accident studies fell during weekends, when the traffic volume was higher. They further claim that the statistical methods used for the homicide rate data are dubious, and when calculated using other methods, the lunar effect is nonexistent. The many studies done by skeptics show no correlation between the moon and human behavior. These skeptics say that the perceived lunar effect is folklore that people want to believe. Further, skeptics assert that because of media hype about the lunar effect, people often assume a causal connection between strange incidents and the full moon.

What Makes People's Joints Click?

When people walk or run, it is common for the joints in their hips or legs to make a clicking sound. It can also occur when people stretch, and some can even purposely make the noise with their fingers. But what causes this clicking sound?

The joints are supported by an array of muscles, tendons, and ligaments, which keep the joints stable. If the tendons or ligaments are out of alignment or slightly lax, the movement of a ligament from one position to another can cause clicking. An example of this is when a ligament flicks over a bone. In this case, the click is caused by the iliotibial band moving over the trochanter. A minor strain in the joint can also cause this.

Another reason for a clicking could be the formation of a vacuum when the joint and muscles move. This vacuum can rapidly fill with gas, forming a bubble that replaces the vacuum. This can cause the joint to click when the joint is then moved. Because it takes a while for the gas to be reabsorbed, the same joint cannot normally be clicked again for a short while.

Most medical professionals agree that, provided there is no pain or swelling associated with the clicking, it is nothing to worry about and can be ignored.

Does an Elephant Truly Never Forget?

It's a common expression that elephants never forget. In fact, one of the collective nouns for a group of elephants is a "memory." The common conception of elephants having great memories has been put to the test over the years by scientists and researchers and found to be true: elephants do have exceptional long-term memories.

An experiment conducted in the 1950s that tested an elephant's recall by showing it various wooden boxes showed that the animal had a remarkable ability to retain information. Many later experiments have produced similar results; in some instances, the testers believe that the elephant uses no particular strategy for recall as some animals do, but instead merely remembers effortlessly. These tests have been backed up by circus-elephant trainers, who have attested to the amazing recall of their animals, asserting that they can learn up to one hundred different commands and remember them for years. Elephants have also been found never to forget someone who has either cared for or mistreated them.

The elephant's incredible memory is particularly acute among the matriarchs who lead the herd. Since the males leave the herd at an early age, it is important for a matriarch to be able to recognize any outsider elephant as friend or foe based on their prior experience of that elephant. Such discrimination enables the rest of the herd to prosper, as they are able to feed and relax without needing to be on the lookout for danger. The matriarch is also able to lead the herd over long distances to places rich with food and water and, in dry times, she is able to find water sources that she has not visited in many years.

Combined with elephants' excellent memory is their high level of general intelligence, as demonstrated in the attention they lavish on their newborn offspring and the way in which they grieve over the losses of loved ones. Indeed, elephants have been known stand vigil over a dead friend and even stop to pay their respects at times when they later pass the place at which the death took place. Elephant herds also have an intricate social structure, which is indicative of intelligent animals.

Do Pregnant Women Really Glow?

How many times have you heard it? "Have you seen her lately? She's pregnant, and really glowing." Is this a popular misconception, or do women really glow when they're pregnant?

Many physiological changes occur to women while they're pregnant, and the pregnancy glow is actually one of them. The glowing effect on a woman's face is caused by a number of factors.

An influx of hormones, particularly progesterone, causes a pregnant woman's glands to produce more oil. This can make the face look shiny, softer, smoother, and more moisturized. During pregnancy, the skin also retains more moisture. This plumps it up, smoothing out fine lines and wrinkles.

Another key contributing factor is an increase in blood flow. During pregnancy, the body increases the production of blood by about 50 percent. This results in more blood circulating closer to the surface of the skin, leading to a brighter, fuller, and more radiant face—the glow.

But it's not all good news. The downsides from glow-contributing factors include hot flashes from the increased blood flow, puffiness from the water retention, and acne from the increased oil production and hormonal changes.

🤔 Why Do Roller Coasters Make You Puke?

People pay good money to go to amusement parks, eager to ride the roller coaster, the key attraction there. The bigger and faster, the better. Minutes later, they feel nauseated and begin puking everywhere. These rides are meant to be fun, so why can roller coasters make even the strongest of people vomit?

Motion sickness is the culprit. Also known as kinetosis, this is the feeling you get when the motion you sense in your inner ear is different from the motion you visually perceive.

Motion sensed in the brain comes from signals sent from the inner ear and the eyes. When we move intentionally, these signals are coordinated in the brain. However, when our movements are unintentional, like they are on a jerking and spinning roller coaster, the brain receives conflicting signals.

The inner ear signals come from the vestibular system. This system consists of canals that contain hairlike sensory nerve cells, as well as a fluid called endolymph. Because of inertia, endolymph resists any change in motion. When we spin around, the endolymph lags behind and stimulates the hairlike cells to signal to the brain that the head is spinning. As the endolymph starts to move at the same rate as you are spinning, it no longer stimulates the hairlike cells, and the brain adapts. When the spinning stops, the endolymph continues to move and this again stimulates the cells, which indicate to the brain that the spinning is still occurring. These incorrect signals contradict what the eyes are telling the brain and cause dizziness, as if you were still spinning. This can result in a feeling of sickness.

But why do we sometimes vomit? There are two biological hypotheses for this unsavory by-product of roller coaster "fun."

When the brain senses a discord between vision and balance, it thinks that the person is hallucinating and that the hallucination is caused by a toxin in the system. As a defense

mechanism to eliminate any dangerous poison, the brain forces the body to vomit.

Another theory is related to the body's fight-or-flight response to danger. When we experience unusual motions and dizziness, the heart pumps faster and redirects blood flow to our vital organs as a survival technique. The body empties its stomach contents so that the blood normally used in the digestion process can also be used by the vital organs.

Various techniques can be adopted to reduce the motion sickness caused by a roller coaster. These include taking regular and controlled breaths, having frequent exposure to the ride in order to increase your tolerance, and using the power of positive thinking—for example, if you think it'll be fun and won't make you sick, a self-fulfilling prophecy may result. But by far, the best way to avoid the feeling of nausea is to sit at the front of the roller coaster. This allows you to better anticipate the changes in direction so that your brain can adapt to them and not be tricked. And sitting at the front has another key advantage: it prevents you from getting covered in the puke from other people.

Why Don't Governments Just Print More Money When They Need It?

When the economy's bad, national debt is high, and nobody has much money to spend, why doesn't the government simply print more money? They have the machines to do it, and it's unlikely anybody would notice anyway. Or would they?

Yes, they would. Wealth isn't created by money; it's only represented by it. When more money is printed without increasing the wealth it represents, each banknote represents a smaller slice of the financial pie. Economic output is not increased in any way, so all that results is inflation. Using a simplistic example, if an economy produces one million items at $10 each and then doubles the amount of money available by printing it, there will still be only one million items available. The demand for the items will rise. They will then be worth $20 each, and nobody will be any better off because their money has devalued.

Inflation in this situation has many negative impacts:

- The value of savings falls.
- It creates uncertainty and confusion, which discourages companies from investing in the economy. This, in turn, leads to lower economic growth.
- Governments borrow money by selling government bonds to the private sector. As bonds are a form of saving, when inflation rises, the value of bonds decreases. To entice investors, the government would have to increase the return on the bonds and would have more difficulty selling them to reduce the national debt.
- Inflation reduces the value of a currency. If prices double and you need twice as much money to buy the same goods, like in the example on the previous page, the purchasing power of the currency will decline against foreign currencies where the inflation is not as high.

A number of examples throughout history show countries printing money to try to solve their financial problems, most notably Germany in the 1920s. To meet the reparations imposed on them after World War I, the German government printed more money. This led to hyperinflation. Money became worthless. So, much was needed to buy goods that some people decided to carry it around in a wheelbarrow. It was said that people would often steal the wheelbarrows but leave the money. Money was even used as wallpaper. The currency fell to extremely low levels, and the economy collapsed. Printing extra money is not a good idea.

Does Bigfoot Exist?

Also known as Sasquatch, Bigfoot is reported to be a large, ape-like animal that lives in the forests of the Rocky Mountains in Canada and the United States. Bigfoot is said to stand about 8 feet tall. It is covered with hair and walks upright on its two hind legs. Although sightings date back to the 1700s, Bigfoot became famous in 1958 when enormous footprints were found in Humboldt County, California.

Footprints have indeed persuaded many to believe in Bigfoot, with some experts arguing that such large, well-spaced prints would be difficult to fake. Tracks found in Washington state in 1969 also suggested that the creature's right foot was crippled. This accorded with a number of eyewitness accounts of Bigfoot's gait. Handprints found in 1970 depicted a large, apelike hand with many irregularities, unlike anything in human anatomy. Indeed, these contained distinct fingerprints common to primates, which law enforcement agencies described as very real. Tested hair samples were also found not to match any known animal species, yet had characteristics common to both humans and animals. However, DNA from all other hair and feces samples have been inconclusive and have not shown that they are from an unknown animal.

A 1967 film of Bigfoot was long considered the most cogent evidence, as the footage was clearly not a bear but an apelike creature walking upright. But a man named Wallace claimed to have been involved in making the film, which he called a hoax. In support of the film, though, is the fact that eyewitness accounts from many different people are strikingly similar, in their descriptions of both the animal and the sounds that it makes.

Despite the array of evidence and sightings, most scientists remain unpersuaded of the Bigfoot phenomenon. Many attribute the sightings to hoaxes or ancient folklore from Native Americans that people want to believe. In addition, there is a lack of fossil evidence, despite there being plentiful fossil evidence of prehistoric bears, cougars, and mammoths. Many experts think the sightings are merely of bears. In fact, in 1997, an Italian mountaineer claimed to have come face-to-face with Bigfoot and eventually shot it. It turned out to be an endangered Himalayan brown bear species that is able to walk upright.

 ## Is Time Travel Possible?

The idea of time travel fascinates humanity. H. G. Wells's novel *The Time Machine* dealt with the concept in 1895, and science fiction writers have been exploring it ever since. Time travel is a fanciful notion, but as science has developed, it has been viewed as increasingly possible. The various theories about how to time travel, which feature wormholes, parallel universes, and spinning cylinders, involve complex, inconclusive mathematical principles.

It is generally accepted that it is impossible to travel back in time to affect an event that has already transpired. To do this would mean recreating every aspect of the universe, including the position of every planet and star, and the exact motion of every molecule at the time. That would be impossible. Similarly, to travel into the future and "suspend animation," so that time passes but the traveler's body is unaffected, is also impossible. There is no way to do this—but some theorists suggest it might be possible.

The kind of time travel that is most frequently debated, and that some scientists now consider a possibility, is going back in time and viewing (although not participating in) the past. Einstein's theories of relativity show how time changes with motion and suggest that, compared with a stationary observer, time appears to pass more slowly for bodies that are moving at a faster speed. Time is not always a constant, and by increasing speed, the passage of time can be altered.

When we look at something, we see the light beams emitted at the time that the light beams are sent. If we could travel faster than the speed of light, perhaps we could overtake the light and see it actually being sent. An example of this is the light given off by the stars. What we see in the sky are the light beams given off years ago, so if we could travel faster than them, we could see them being emitted and see the event that they are emitting. In other words, we would view a past event by overtaking the light beams that carried that event. Although this time travel is possible in theory, it would mean traveling faster than 186,000 miles per second. This is not possible at present, and there is no experimental evidence to indicate that it ever will be possible. It is all theory.

Do You Get Wetter When Walking in the Rain Than You Do When Running?

The question of whether people will get wetter if they walk through the rain than if they run through it has been the subject of much barroom discussion. In fact, scientists have been considering the problem for many years, and have concluded that many factors can contribute to which method of progress exposes a person to more rain. Some factors are the speed and intensity of the rain, the build of the person, the direction and angle of the rain, and the distance traveled.

The main reason for the debate is the fact that raindrops generally hit both the head and the front of the body. It has been thought that because a runner will be in the rain for a shorter period than a walker will, fewer drops will hit his or her head, and this is a generally agreed-upon hypothesis. However, some believe that a runner will be hit

with more drops on the front of the body because of his or her increased velocity when running. The balance of these two factors has been put to the test scientifically.

A number of experiments have been performed to determine the best way of keeping dry when moving in the rain, most of which have resulted in a running person ending up less wet than a walking person. While some experiments found that the number of drops per second that a runner received was the same as for a walker (because the runner was hit more on the front but less on the head), the runner was in the rain for a shorter period and so got hit with fewer drops overall. A number of experiments counting the actual number of drops that hit both a runner and a walker found that the runner received far fewer head drops, but that the front drops for the runner and walker were the same, which again resulted in the runner getting less wet.

In one experiment, the runner ended up getting 40 percent less wet, while in another this figure was reduced to 10 percent. A 1997 experiment found that running in a light rain with no wind resulted in the runner getting 16 percent less wet, while leaning forward and running fast in heavy rain being driven by wind resulted in the runner getting 44 percent less wet. On the basis of these experiments, it's possible to determine that running is always the best option, particularly in heavy rain.

❓ Can a Cockroach Survive a Nuclear Bomb?

Cockroaches are resilient creatures that have lived on Earth for 300 million years, predating the dinosaurs by 150 million years. After atomic bombs were dropped on Hiroshima and Nagasaki in 1945, reports later emerged that the only survivors in those cities were cockroaches, whose populations seemed largely unaffected. This led many to believe that roaches can survive nuclear bombs. So, can they, or is this just another urban myth?

To test this theory, various scientific teams have conducted experiments on cockroaches over the last 60 years, exposing them to the radioactive metal cobalt 60, a synthetic substance produced artificially in nuclear reactors. After an exposure of 1,000 radon units (rads), which was the level of radiation detected about 15 miles from Hiroshima directly after the bomb was detonated and is capable of killing a person in 10 minutes, most cockroaches survived, although their fertility was severely compromised. After exposure to 10,000 rads, the amount of radiation emitted by the Hiroshima bomb, only one in ten cockroaches survived, and at a level of 100,000 rads, no cockroaches lived.

The ability of cockroaches to withstand extreme radiation owes to the simple design of their bodies and their relatively slow cell cycles. Cells are most sensitive to radiation when they're dividing. The cells of a cockroach divide about every two days, and the insects molt only once a week. The cells of humans, on the other hand, are constantly changing and renewing, making us 10 times more susceptible to radiation than cockroaches.

Cockroaches, however, are nuclear lightweights compared with others in the insect world. It takes 64,000 rads to kill the fruit fly, 100,000 rads to kill the flour beetle, and the *Habrobracon hebetor*, a type of parasitic wasp, can withstand an astonishing 180,000 rads.

In short, while cockroaches would not be able to withstand the direct impact of an explosion, some would be able to survive the radiation produced by a blast on the level of the Hiroshima bomb. They wouldn't survive the far more powerful bombs of today, but they're still impressively hardy bugs. This begs the question: Just how strong is the stuff they put in bug spray, anyway?

What Causes Songs to Get Stuck in Our Heads?

You're driving to work listening to the radio, when Lady Gaga's "Poker Face" comes on. By the time you make it to work, you're singing her incredibly catchy chorus in your head over and over. This lasts all day; you hum it, tap it out on the desk, and sing the song repeatedly until it drives you crazy. Sound familiar? What causes a tune like this to get stuck in our heads, forcing us to play it over and over and over again?

It's an earworm. Sometimes known as stuck song syndrome, an earworm is a catchy piece of music that plays in a continuous loop in a person's mind long after they stop listening to the song. The term is translated from the German word *ohrwurm*. Ninety-nine percent of people fall victim to earworms on a regular basis.

Music cognition research suggests that earworms are related to the brain's motor cortex. There is a lot of activity in that part of the brain when people listen to music, and the brain often sings along as an imaginary participant. The problem is that the brain keeps singing long after the music stops.

Earworms tend to be a small fragment or chorus of a song, about 15 to 30 seconds long, and are usually songs we've been repeatedly exposed to recently. However, they can also be caused by experiences that trigger the memory of a song. The songs usually have simple and repetitive lyrics and an upbeat melody, but with an unexpected variation in rhythm that piques the listener's interest—essentially, the same factors that make certain pop songs and jingles successful in the first place. Songs with lyrics account for the vast majority of earworms.

Most people are doing something routine and not concentrating on a particular task when earworms strike. You are also more likely to get one when you're stressed, tired, or idle, and research has found that people who are neurotic or obsessive compulsive experience them more often.

So, what's the point of these persistent little critters? Some experts claim they assist in emotional regulation, while others suggest they are a way of keeping an idle brain busy. There is also the suggestion that earworms have an evolutionary origin.

Before writing was invented, songs helped people to remember and then share information. Supporting this theory is the fact that when people sing their earworms aloud, they are usually a surprisingly close match to the original song in terms of pitch, key, and rhythm.

Given that we can now write stuff down and don't have to rely on melodic mnemonics, how do we get rid of an earworm? That's the problem: they're notoriously difficult to dislodge, and the harder we try to suppress them, the more entrenched they often become. They usually crawl out on their own eventually, but some proven cures are to sing or listen to another song, do an activity that involves more concentration, or listen to the entire song a few times in an attempt to exhaust it. One study suggested that chewing gum might also help. Whatever you do, don't tell a friend about it, as that'll give them the same earworm, and they'll hate you for the rest of the day.

So, which songs cause the most earworms? "Don't Worry, Be Happy" and "I Will Survive" are commonly cited as two of the biggest culprits. Kylie Minogue's "Can't Get You out of My Head" is also a repeat offender—it's so bad, in fact, that she wrote a song about it.

Is It True That You Can't Die in a Dream?

Many people have dreams in which they are about to die, but then they wake up just before their death occurs. This has led some to believe that you can't actually die in your dreams. Is there any basis to this, or is it an urban myth?

According to the International Association for the Study of Dreams, the idea that you can't die in your dreams, or that if you do you would have to die in real life as well, is a complete myth. They claim that many people have dreamed of their deaths and lived to tell the tale.

But there is another, more philosophical argument against the idea. To know that you are dead in your dream, you would have to be viewing the event, which means that you wouldn't be dead. Only the character you are "playing" in the dream can die, and not you as a spectator. Technically, this means you cannot die in a dream, but it is a fine line.

Many people report waking up before dying, but never actually dying in a dream. The reason this happens could be that people don't really understand what happens when our bodies die, and, as we have obviously never personally experienced death in real life, our minds do not have enough information to complete the event in a dream.

When interpreting dreams of death that do occur, some psychologists and dream experts say these dreams symbolically signify the ending of something in your actual life, such as a relationship. Others claim they are a positive thing, symbolizing inner changes or a transformation that is about to take place in your life.

One thing is for sure: if you do die in a dream, it doesn't mean that you have to actually die or are about to die in real life. So, whether you die in your dreams or not, don't lose too much sleep over it.

Why Do People Look Upward When Thinking?

Ask someone a difficult question, and chances are they will either close their eyes or look up to the sky. Why is this so?

As with many conundrums such as this, there are a number of theories.

Many people use visualization to answer questions. If the eyes are open and receiving additional input, it is harder to concentrate and visualize the answer because the brain is busy dealing with the new information the eyes are seeing. People also have difficulty doing more than one thing at a time, so if they close their eyes or look upward, they are able to eliminate distractions and disengage from the world. By doing this, they can more easily access memories or focus their attention on the problem at hand.

This distraction theory was supported by a 2011 study by Annelies Vredeveldt, Graham Hitch, and Alan Baddeley at the University of York in England. Subjects watched a television show and were then asked questions about what they had seen and heard. One group answered the questions while looking at a blank computer screen, while a second group answered with their eyes closed. A third group answered while watching a computer screen when images were shown on it, and the fourth group was distracted by a foreign language while they answered the questions. The people from the groups who looked at the blank screen or closed their eyes had far better recall than the people from the two groups who were distracted.

A second, more controversial theory to explain why people look up when they're thinking was postulated in the 1960s by a Canadian psychologist named Paul Bakan. He postulated that different types of thinking triggered lateral eye movements, also known as LEMs. When right-handed people are visualizing constructed events (that is, lying), they access the creative part of their brain and tend to look up and to the right. When they are recalling an actual memory (that is, being honest), they access the memory center of their brain and tend to look up and to the left. It is the opposite for left-handers.

This theory has been widespread for years, but a number of subsequent studies on LEMs have proved inconclusive. In 2012, a comprehensive three-part study on the topic was undertaken by Professor Richard Wiseman of the University of Hertfordshire in England. He found that there was no relationship between lying and eye movements.

If Wiseman is right, the probable reason that people look upward when thinking is to aid in concentration by eliminating distractions. But maybe they're just looking for a skywriter to give them a believable response.

❓ What's the Difference between a Turtle and a Tortoise?

Tortoises and turtles look very similar. They are both encased in a hard shell, and both possess reptilian characteristics, such as breathing air, being cold-blooded, laying their eggs on dry land, and having scales. They are both reptiles from the order of Testudines but are in different classification families. A lot of

Tortoise   *Sea turtle*

people confuse the two animals, leading some to ponder, how do you tell them apart?

There are three main differences.

1. The key difference is that tortoises dwell on land, while turtles live in water most or all of the time, usually only coming on to land to lay eggs.

2. Because of their different habitats, the animals have adapted differently. Turtles have either webbed feet or long flippers, both of which aid in swimming. Their shells are flatter and hug their bodies more. Tortoises, on the other hand, are not good swimmers and have stubby, column-shaped feet that assist them in traveling across land. They are not as streamlined as turtles and have high, domed shells. They also have sharp claws that they use to dig burrows for sleeping or shelter.

3. Turtles are omnivores. Sea turtles eat small invertebrates as well as sea vegetation, and freshwater turtles eat plants, small fish, and insects. Tortoises are herbivores, eating grasses, low-lying shrubs, weeds, and other vegetation.

Actually, there's one other major difference. While tortoises are known to compete in endurance races against sleepy hares, when turtles reach their teenage years, they often mutate and develop highly advanced ninja skills.

What Is a Black Hole?

Don't let the name deceive you—a black hole is the opposite of empty space. It's only called that because we can't see it. And here's why.

A black hole is a place in space where the gravity is so strong that nothing can escape it, not even light. When a star gets to the end of its life cycle, its gravity can become so powerful that it collapses in upon itself, producing a supernova explosion. Fragments of the star scatter through space, but a small and dense core will remain and compress into a smaller space. If the core's mass is large and dense enough (at least three times the size of the sun), its gravity will be so strong that a black hole develops, from which nothing can escape. The black hole can then continue to grow by using its gravity to absorb additional mass from its surroundings.

Black holes vary in size, from a stellar black hole that can be twenty times the mass of the sun, to a supermassive black hole that can reach a mass the size of millions of suns. Scientists believe there are as many as a billion stellar black holes in the Milky Way alone (which is the earth's galaxy), and they have discovered a supermassive black hole at its center, called Sagittarius A. It has a mass equal to four million suns.

So, given that we can't see them, and no light can escape from them, how do we know they're there?

Scientists are able to detect black holes by watching their effects on other stars and gases. Nearby stars may be sucked into a black hole, or, if far enough away, orbit the black hole. As a star is drawn toward a black hole, it accelerates and heats up, emitting X-rays that scientists can see.

The term was first used in 1964, but the concept of black holes has been around for centuries, and Einstein discussed them in his theory of general relativity. But the key question is, could the earth be sucked into one?

No. The sun is not big enough to turn into a black hole, and there are no other black holes close enough to affect us.

❓ Why Don't We Eat Horsemeat?

Known as hippophagy, the eating of horsemeat has been practiced across the world for centuries. Still today, many countries consider horse a delicacy, and it is widely available in Asia and parts of Europe, where it outsells mutton and lamb.

Horsemeat is good for you. It's a good source of protein, has a sweet flavor, is tender, contains fewer calories than beef, and has a lot more omega-3 fatty acids than beef. And it's not as if horses are unavailable or too expensive. The United States has hundreds of thousands of excess horses that are either abandoned by owners who can't afford them or are running wild and damaging their environment.

Yet, since the turn of this century, many laws have been passed throughout the United States effectively banning the slaughter of horses for human consumption.

As a nation, Americans eat a lot of meat, but not horsemeat. Why the uproar?

The reason is thought to stem back to AD 732, when Pope Gregory III decreed that the ritual consumption of horsemeat was a pagan practice that had to be eliminated. He described hippophagy as a "filthy and abominable custom." Some historians believe that he was trying to preserve horses for warfare, but whatever the reason, the papal ban was effective and dissuaded people from eating horses for centuries.

The residual impact of that decree may have had some influence in the United States over the years, but the real reason

Americans don't eat horsemeat is because we love our beasts of burden. Horses have long been a sort of mythological creature in the American national consciousness. From the time they were brought to US shores by the Spanish in the 16th century, they were highly valued by Native Americans for warfare and hunting. Horses were later essential to the exploration of the American frontier and were instrumental in shaping the nation. Many people relish the image of a cowboy traveling across America, the horse as their trusted companion. Horses were then used as valuable workers and as transportation, and later as pets. To many Americans, eating a horse is taboo and would be like eating a cat or a dog.

It seems that's the end of the matter for now. So, while there is an abundance of horses available for slaughter, and horsemeat is cheap, tasty, and good for you, most Americans say, "Nay, nay, we just don't want to eat our friends."

Does Listening to Mozart Really Make Babies Smarter?

During a woman's pregnancy, you should play one of Mozart's symphonies loudly enough for the unborn baby to hear it, or better still, place some headphones on the mother's stomach. Because of what is known as the Mozart Effect, it is a popular idea that playing classical musical to an unborn child will make them smarter. But is there any science to back up this suggestion?

French researcher Dr. Alfred A. Tomatis first described the Mozart Effect in his 1991 book, *Pourquoi Mozart?* In it, he explored thirty years of research on the music of Mozart's ability to help mentally disabled children. Then, in 1993, a paper published in the journal *Nature* detailed an experiment where thirty-six college students were asked to undertake several spatial reasoning tasks. The students who had listened to ten minutes of Mozart beforehand performed better than those who hadn't. While the study was limited to spatial intelligence, that is an accepted indicator of IQ. This result, as well as the fact that Mozart was the only music listened to in the study, led to the association of his music with intelligence. The Mozart Effect then received traction in a number of newspaper articles, with Alex Ross, a music columnist for the *New York Times*, notably reporting in 1994 that "listening to Mozart actually makes you smarter."

That's how it started, but is it true? Don Campbell, the author of numerous books dealing with music, health, and education, believes that music has a tremendous organizing influence on the brain and can modulate moods, as well as alleviate stress. "I know it improves our ability to be intelligent," he has said. However, "a meta-analysis of a number of Mozart Effect studies was undertaken in 1999 by Christopher Chabris, a psychologist at Union College in Schenectady, New York." He found that listening to Mozart only slightly improved people's spatial skills and nothing else. Further, there is no evidence that classical music played to babies, pre- or post-natally, increases their intelligence or helps with cognitive abilities in any way.

Apart from the lack of evidence, critics cite that if parents are playing classical music to their babies and these babies turn out to be intelligent, it's probably more related to the fact that parents who listen to classical music are more likely to be intelligent themselves, and so produce smarter babies.

So, if you like Mozart's music, by all means keep listening to it, but don't expect it to turn your baby into a genius.

How Did the Term "Blackmail" Originate?

To blackmail is to extort money from someone, usually by the threat of exposing a damaging secret.

The word "blackmail" originated in the Scottish Highlands in the 17th century. The "mail" in the word comes from the Scottish *male*, meaning rent or tax. Farmers paid their usual rent in silver coins, which was known as white money, probably because of the light color of the silver. But farmers who lived along the remote Scottish-English border, away from the cities and larger towns, were subjected to a further tax.

The Highland clan chiefs set up a protection scheme. They threatened the locals with violence or theft of livestock if the farmers did not pay money to be protected from the other clans. This additional payment became known as black male, as opposed to the legitimate payment of white male.

By the 1900s, blackmail had developed the wider meaning that it has today.

Do Bees Die after They Sting You?

A bee can only sting once, and when it does, it dies. Kids have been spouting this fact for decades, but is there any truth in it?

It depends on the type of bee. The stinger on a bee or wasp is a type of ovipositor (that is, an organ for depositing eggs). It is only female bees that sting; they inject venom into the victim through a stylus that is enclosed between a pair of lancets.

When a bee or wasp stings you, the lancets become embedded in your skin.

In most bees and wasps, the lancets are fairly smooth, with only tiny barbs. After stinging, these barbs are easily retracted, and the stinger can be removed.

However, in honeybees, the stinger is large and has barbs that face backward. When the honeybee stings, these barbs lodge under a person's skin, and the bee is unable to remove its stinger. As the bee tries to free the stinger and fly away, the stinger is torn from the bee's body, removing its abdomen and digestive tract, as well as some muscles and nerves. This abdominal rupture kills the bee.

The bee will only die if the skin of the animal it stings is sufficiently thick, preventing removal of the lancets and causing the abdominal rupture. So, a honeybee would normally be able to sting an insect and live to sting again, but not a human.

So, when a honeybee stings you, that is indeed the final act of its life. You may take some satisfaction in knowing that, but beware, as the bee often has the last laugh. In addition to the

stinger, the bee's venom sacs are also left behind. If you squeeze the stinger to try to get it out, as many people do, it pumps even more poison into your body.

Why Does Seeing Food Make Your Mouth Water?

Picture a tender, juicy steak accompanied by salty fries straight out of the oven. Or a rich piece of chocolate cake with thick icing. Is your mouth watering yet? What causes our mouths to water whenever we see or smell, or even think of, delicious food?

Saliva plays an important role in eating and digestion. It lubricates the food we eat, helping us to work it around in our mouths for chewing. It also contains enzymes that start the digestion process. These enzymes help start breaking down the food in the mouth, well before it reaches the stomach.

When we see or smell delicious food, the brain processes these senses, sending a signal to the salivary glands to produce the saliva in preparation for eating. The brain anticipates the fact that the food will be eaten, and as a reflex action, produces saliva in advance, allowing us to eat immediately. This would have been particularly important for our ancestors, who might have had to eat quickly after making a kill before scavenging predators arrived on the scene.

In fact, one of the enzymes in our saliva is called salivary amylase, which breaks down starches. Humans carry extra copies of the gene that encodes this enzyme, and scientists believe this may have helped to hasten human evolution. Humans carry as many as fifteen copies of the gene, compared to chimpanzees, who only have two. We probably developed more to deal with a changing diet in early humans that may have fueled an increase in the size of human brains and bodies.

The term "mouthwatering" is actually very accurate. There are two types of saliva, mucous and serous. Mucous saliva is thick and sticky, while serous saliva is very watery. It is this serous saliva that floods your mouth at the smell or sight of particularly ambrosial food.

Is It Dangerous to Wake a Sleepwalker?

Many of us have heard over the years that whatever you do, don't wake someone who is sleepwalking. Sleepwalking puts a person in such a strange state that if they are woken, the shock they experience can have serious consequences for the sleepwalker, including a heart attack or brain damage.

This is a myth. Despite the urban legend, waking a sleepwalker is harmless. It is no different from waking someone who is sleeping normally. They might get a shock, but that's about it.

This shock, however, could be dangerous for the person waking up the sleepwalker. Sleepwalking occurs during stage 3 non-rapid eye movement sleep, also known as slow-wave sleep. This stage of sleep is very deep, so waking a person from it is not only difficult but, once done, can leave a person in a state of cognitive impairment for up to thirty minutes. This may result in the sleepwalker waking in a startled, confused, or agitated state. Not immediately recognizing you as someone they know may cause them to strike out at you. For your own safety, it is best not to rouse a sleepwalker, but to simply guide them back to bed in their sleep.

According to the National Sleep Foundation, sleepwalking is completely normal and is very common, with an estimated 15 percent of the United States population doing it, generally between the ages of four and six.

So where did the myth that waking a sleepwalker could kill them originate? Dr. Mark Mahowald, an expert in sleeping and sleep disorders at Stanford University, has cited an ancient belief that a person's soul can leave their body while they are asleep. Should that person then be awoken while sleepwalking, it would mean that they would have to walk forever without a soul.

And the most common sleepwalking behavior? Urination. People have gotten out of bed and peed in a cupboard, in a shoe, or anywhere else that's not the toilet. What's more, as sleepwalking generally occurs in an unconscious state, the perpetrator will have no recollection of the indiscretion.

Is It Possible for Robots to Think for Themselves?

Is the dreaded science fiction scenario possible? Humans are subjugated to robots, following their every command as they rule the world, self-improve, and do whatever they like.

While this sounds unrealistic, experts say that advances in technology may have made the thinking robot possible.

Until recently, humans have operated robots by either remote control or specific verbal commands that the robot is programmed to compute. But now, increasingly autonomous machines, such as toys or vacuum cleaners that clean the room alone without needing any human instructions, are available.

Manufacturers predict that this sort of machine will advance further in the coming years, so that robots are able to mind children and work in care homes and prisons, transmitting their progress to humans via built-in cameras.

Some incredible robots already exist. A software system known as Deep Q-Networks has been programmed to play Atari games such as *Space Invaders*. The system is able to learn directly from its experience using trial and error, without further human interaction.

Then there's the Hasegawa Group at the Tokyo Institute of Technology. Using a technology called "Self-Organizing Incremental Neural Network," they have created robots that are capable of learning for themselves when they encounter problems that they have never seen before. The robots make educated guesses and decisions based on their experiences, enabling them to adapt to new situations. They then store that knowledge, effectively increasing their intelligence.

That all might sound pretty scary, but robots are still just tools designed for a specific purpose. It is possible to write programs that mimic human thought, allowing a robot to recognize and respond to patterns, but it is still simply responding to commands, and the ability to give a robot consciousness—emotions and the free will to improve its own design—is beyond our grasp. It may be that consciousness can never be artificially simulated.

So, if you live in constant fear of the day that humans become redundant and robots take over the world, you're okay—for now, anyway. But you might want to treat your computer a little better, just in case.

❓ Why Do Beans Make You Fart?

"Baked beans are good for your heart; baked beans make you fart." So the catchy playground rhyme goes.

A can of baked beans is a good source of vegetable protein, as well as minerals such as potassium, magnesium, zinc, copper, calcium, and phosphorus. Beans are also low in fat, contain a number of vitamins, and are high in soluble fiber, which is beneficial for the digestive system. They're super quick and easy to prepare, as well. So, what's the catch?

They make you fart. Baked beans contain carbohydrates called oligosaccharides, a category that includes raffinose and stachyose. These carbohydrates give beans their natural sweetness, but they are made of molecules that are too large for our small intestine to absorb during the digestion process. Instead, the molecules pass through to the lower intestine.

It is the bacteria in that larger intestine that thrives on these molecules, breaking them down. As this metabolic process takes place, large amounts of gases are produced as a by-product, principally hydrogen, nitrogen, and carbon dioxide. These gases accumulate and escape the body as flatulence.

To reduce the amount of oligosaccharides in beans, they can be boiled and washed first. Another way to reduce gas is by taking an alpha-galactosidase supplement, such as Beano. The alpha-galactosidase enzyme breaks down the molecules, enabling them to be absorbed in the small intestine.

Failing that, just keep doing what you're doing and blame it on the dog.

Why Do People Seem More Attractive When You're Drunk?

The plight of the 21st-century single male might sound familiar to some: You've been drinking all night when suddenly the bar is filled with gorgeous women. It looks like a model's convention in there, and the girl you're talking to really is beautiful. You look at her sparkling eyes and her winning smile. She's irresistible. You ask her home and she agrees. You can't believe your luck! That is, until you wake up the next day. "Surely, this isn't the girl I took home. This one could scare a hungry dog out of a butcher's shop. What was I thinking? What happened?" What happened was your "beer goggles," the ultimate societal curse.

The phenomenon known as beer goggles means that the more alcohol you drink, the more attractive you find the opposite sex. Some say that it is just a myth, and alcohol merely suppresses people's inhibitions, making them less discriminating and more likely to approach strangers. Science says otherwise.

Results of a study done at the University of Bristol in England showed that a group of college students found members of the opposite sex 10 percent more attractive after drinking only two beers. Another study, done at the University of Glasgow and the University of St. Andrews, both in Scotland, found that students who had consumed a moderate amount of alcohol found the faces of members of the opposite sex 25 percent more attractive than when they were sober.

The leading theory as to what causes beer goggles is related to bilateral symmetry. One of the predominant factors of beauty is symmetry. A perfectly symmetrical face is generally found to be good-looking. This is because symmetry is a sign of health, suggesting that the person is free from disease and deformation. In simple terms, the more similar one side of a person's face is to the other side, the better looking that person is. A series of studies suggests that alcohol impairs our ability to perceive asymmetry, making us find asymmetrical faces far more attractive when drunk than when sober. So, it's not that our standards drop, but that our brain genuinely finds people more attractive during the time of intoxication.

But it's not just as simple as getting drunk to increase your chances—beer goggles do not bring success if applied unilaterally. To reap the benefits of the phenomenon, your target must also be drunk. Fortunately, the goggles fit both sexes. Note of caution: Studies have also found that beer goggles make the same sex seem more attractive, as well.

Are Bulls Really Attracted to the Color Red?

Bullfighting has been a tradition in Spain, France, and some Latin American countries for centuries. The matadors use a small red cape, known as a muleta, in the latter part of the fight, and the bull goes mad, charging at it repeatedly. Why does the color red make these animals so angry?

It doesn't. The bull is actually charging at the movement of the cape, not its color. Bulls, along with all bovines, are color-blind to red, but they are bred to be aggressive and to charge any moving object. Tests have shown that bulls prefer to charge a person who is moving rather than someone who is stationary, regardless of the color they are wearing. The matadors entice the bull to charge by waving the red cape at it. This movement infuriates the bull and it charges. And the bulls will charge any color. In the early stages of the fight, the matador uses a larger magenta- and gold-colored cape, and the bull charges that with equal fury.

So, if a bull can't see red, why is the muleta red?

The ornate costumes of the matadors and the red capes that they use are all part of the spectacle, and have been since bullfighting began. They are considered an important part of the culture and tradition of bullfighting.

There is also a practical reason for the cape's color. The red helps mask the bull's blood.

 ## Is There Life on Mars?

Whether there is life on Mars is a question that scientists have speculated about for centuries. The obsession with life on Mars is probably because of its relatively close proximity to Earth and also because of the similarities between the two planets. In the 1600s, polar ice caps were observed on Mars. By the 1800s, astronomers had determined that the length of a day on Mars is similar to the length of a day on Earth. Its axial tilt is also similar to that of Earth, meaning that seasons exist on Mars. H. G. Wells's 1897 novel *The War of the Worlds*, which describes an invasion by Martians, also fueled the speculation.

In the past century, scientists observed that Mars is an arid land, exposed to harsh cosmic radiation because of its lack of a shielding magnetic field. These factors made life on Mars seem very unlikely. However, speculation has increased in recent years, owing to a number of significant findings. Evidence of water under the surface of Mars has been discovered, and in March 2004, scientists at NASA concluded that Mars was once a wet planet, capable of sustaining life. An orbiting probe near Mars then discovered methane gas in the Martian atmosphere. Methane could not last for more than a few hundred years without being replenished, and could be formed only by volcanic activity or by a life-form metabolizing hydrogen and carbon dioxide to produce methane (on Earth, organisms called methanogens do this). No volcanoes have been discovered on Mars, and in 2005, a group of scientists from the European Space Agency reported that the methane was of organic origin, suggesting life on Mars. At the conference where these findings were reported, 75 percent of the delegates agreed that life once existed on Mars, and 25 percent believed that there is still life on Mars today.

Shortly after methane was found in the atmosphere of Mars, ammonia was also found. Ammonia would disappear within hours if it were not replenished. It is a compound of nitrogen and hydrogen, and although nitrogen is rare on Mars, no life can exist without it. This has led more scientists to believe that there are currently life-forms on Mars.

Why Didn't People Smile in Old Photos?

Historical accounts say that Charles Darwin was very friendly, Abraham Lincoln had a humorous persona, and Mark Twain was armed with a sharp wit. But anybody looking at photographs of these three would assume they were the most serious and gloomy men who ever lived. In the photos of today, people smile and laugh, desperate to show how happy and social they are. Why did our ancestors appear so disconsolate when being photographed?

Some claim that people of yesteryear froze in their photos to allow for the longer exposure times in the cameras, or that they didn't want to show off their rotting teeth. Both of these suggestions are unlikely. And while times were often financially harder when photography began, it's not as if laughter and mirth did not exist—carnivals and court jesters were the order of the day, so people loved to have a good time.

The reasons lie in the attitudes to both smiling and portraiture that existed in that era.

While today we think of smiles as being an indication of humor and happiness, in the 1800s it was believed that people who smiled a lot were poor, drunk, or simple. Those of higher standing and character did not readily smile in public.

In addition to that, it was traditional for people not to smile when having their portrait painted. In the early days of photography, having a photograph taken was not dissimilar to having a portrait done—it was a rare occurrence, and for many people, it was a once-in-a-lifetime experience. People understood being photographed as a significant moment, intended as a timeless record of a person, much like a painted portrait was. Technology had given people  the chance to be "painted" like a king, and they took it very seriously. As Mark Twain once wrote, "A photograph is a most important document, and there is nothing more damning to go down to posterity than a silly, foolish smile caught and fixed forever."

The question then becomes, Why did we start smiling in photos?

By the early 1900s, in an attempt to associate their products with happiness and good times, companies used pictures of smiling models in their marketing campaigns. Kodak was no exception. They advertised heavily with smiling models, emphasizing the pleasure of the photograph. People soon began smiling in photos and the trend continued to modern times.

Why Is a Dollar Called a "Buck"?

Here in the United States, and other countries where the unit of currency is the dollar, the slang term "buck" is often used in its place. The most popular theory of the word's origin is that it derives from the Native American bartering of goods in the 18th century. At that time, the hide of a male deer—buckskin—was a common bartering item. The term was later shortened to "buck" and, as the bartering system was gradually replaced with a system of monetary exchange, the word came to be a reference for a dollar. Some people argue, however, that a dollar wasn't referred to as a buck until well after the bartering system had been replaced, also claiming that one buckskin was worth far more than one dollar.

Another possible origin of the word "buck" is as an early gambling term. When gambling was first practiced, a marker was used to determine whose turn it was to deal, and this marker was known as a "buck," because it was usually a buck knife, with a handle fashioned from buck horn. A silver dollar was said to be used later as the marker, but the term "buck" remained.

Why Don't Tornadoes Hit Big Cities?

When most people picture a tornado in their minds, they see the menacing signature spiral snaking its way across the plains, destroying everything in its path. But why are they always going across open countryside? Why don't they hit big cities?

They do. It's a common myth that tornadoes don't strike city areas. One basis for the myth is the argument that the tall skyscrapers in cities could affect the airflow patterns needed to sustain a tornado, but there is little basis for this. Tornadoes can reach 9 miles in height and over a mile across. Such supercells would not be repelled by the buildings of a city.

The fact is that cities don't get hit as often as other areas because of their small size. Cities make up a very small percentage of the land compared to the open, less populated areas of the country.

Climate plays the biggest role in whether a tornado forms or not. The Midwest, known as Tornado Alley, receives an abundance of warm, moist air from the Gulf of Mexico, warm and dry air from the west, and cool air from the north. The combination of these three types of air is perfect for tornado formation and is far different from the conditions on the east or west coasts, where population densities are higher in large cities like New York and Los Angeles. Within Tornado Alley, the population density is low and the cities are smaller, so the chances of a tornado hitting a city are low.

While the odds of a city being hit are low, tornadoes can travel anywhere, and cities do get hit. Both Dallas and Miami were hit in 1997, while Los Angeles has had thirty tornadoes since 1918. There are numerous other examples, including St. Louis. This large city in Missouri, right in the midst of Tornado Alley, has a long history of destructive tornadoes and has been hit numerous times in the past fifty years.

❓ How Did April Fool's Day Originate?

The first of April is known as April Fool's Day, when it's customary to play tricks and pranks on people, although superstition dictates that the pranking ends at noon and any pranks after that time will bring bad luck to the prankster. Anyone who fails to take a joke in good humor is also said to be cursed with bad luck for the following year.

It's not known exactly why this date is recognized in this way or why jokes are played on people. One theory is that it is related to the arrival of spring, when nature "fools" the world with its temperamental weather, while another theory is that it is to celebrate the fruitless journey of the rook that was sent from Noah's Ark in an attempt to find land.

The most widely held view of the origins of April Fool's Day is that it began in the late 16th century, when the Gregorian calendar replaced the Julian calendar. In the old Julian calendar, the year began on March 25, and festivals marking the start of the new year took place on April 1, because March 25 fell during the Christian Holy Week. When the Gregorian calendar changed the new year to begin on January 1, however, the day continued to be recognized. It is believed that forgetful people who could be tricked into continuing to celebrate the new year on April 1 after the calendar had been changed were known as "April Fools." On this date, people would invite others to nonexistent parties and events, pretending that the parties were new year's celebrations.

Nowadays, in England the victim of a prank on April 1 is called an "April Fool," while in Scotland he or she is known as a "gowk," which means a fool or cuckoo. French people who fall foul of fooling on April 1 are known as *poissons d'avril*, which translates as "April fish."

Why Are Typewriter Keys Arranged the Way They Are?

The keys of typewriters are arranged in a specific fashion, with the letters QWERTY being the first six letters of the top row of letters. The 1874 Sholes & Glidden typewriters established the QWERTY layout, which had been patented by Christopher Sholes in 1868. The home-row keys of ASDFGHJKL suggest that the QWERTY keyboard began as an alphabetical design and developed from there. Sholes originally experimented with an array of different keyboard layouts, and there are several theories about why he eventually settled on the QWERTY design.

The QWERTY layout is generally considered inefficient because of the distance the fingers have to move to hit the most commonly used keys. Many believe this was done intentionally to slow the typist's fingers and keep the machine from jamming. The

incidence of jamming was further reduced because commonly used combinations of letters were placed apart from each other. This prevented the typebars of the letters in these combinations from clashing with each other and becoming stuck.

QWERTY also attempted to alternate common letters within combinations between the typist's hands, so that, as one hand was typing the first letter of a combination, the second hand could be in place for the second letter, thereby increasing typing speed somewhat without increasing the risk of jamming.

Because "typewriter" is one of the longest words that can be typed using a single row of the QWERTY keyboard (the top row), some suggest that the sales staff designed the layout so that they could quickly type the word to impress customers. But most experts think this an unlikely reason for QWERTY.

Although most of these potential reasons are inapplicable today, modern computer keyboards have maintained the traditional layout despite various attempts to introduce more efficient designs.

What's the Origin of the "Six Degrees of Separation" Theory?

Six degrees of separation is the theory that every person in the world can be connected to any other person through a chain of no more than five other people. It does seem a little far-fetched that the Queen of England knows someone, who knows someone, and the person only three steps later knows a child who's living in a mud hut in Africa. What are the chances?

Actually, very high.

The theory was first proposed in 1929 by the Hungarian writer Frigyes Karinthy in a short story called "Chains." Then, in the 1950s, Ithiel de Sola Pool from MIT and Manfred Kochen from IBM set out to prove it mathematically. They were unable to fully prove the theory, and it wasn't until 1967, with an experiment devised by the American sociologist Stanley Milgram, that it was properly put to the test. Milgram gave the name, occupation, and general location of a group of people who lived in Massachusetts to a separate group of randomly selected people from the Midwest. These people were asked to send a package to anyone they knew personally, who they believed was the most likely to know the recipient. The person they sent it to would do the same, and so on, until the package was delivered. Most people expected the chain to include hundreds of people, but on average, it took only five to seven intermediaries for each package to be successfully delivered.

Milgram's findings, entitled "The Small World Problem," were published in Psychology Today, a popular science journal. The article generated enormous publicity for the experiments and the phrase "six degrees of separation" was soon born.

Milgram's theory was tested on the internet by Duncan Watts, a professor at Columbia University, in 2001. The "package" in the study was an email, which was sent by 48,000 people to 19 recipients. Watts discovered that the average number of intermediaries was indeed six.

It is unlikely that Stanley Milgram knew what sort of impact his experiment was going to have on today's culture when he started it in 1967. He was probably also not thinking about a nine-year-old Pennsylvanian boy who would later inspire so many discussions on the topic that a game was developed in his honor—Six Degrees of Kevin Bacon.

Why Can't We Remember Our Early Childhood?

Most people suffer from a condition known as childhood amnesia, in which the memories from early childhood are either nonexistent or very hazy. Quite often, they don't exist, but we construct them from photos or stories told to us. While nearly everyone experiences this phenomenon, it still puzzles psychologists, and the explanation for it is not clear. There are four hypotheses, and most scientists agree that one, or a combination of them, is the likely cause.

1. **An Underdeveloped Brain.** The infant brain isn't developed enough to form long-term memories. The hippocampus, which is the part of the brain responsible for forming memories, is fairly developed by the age of one, but continues developing until at least the age of seven. The prefrontal cortex, which scientists believe helps us to form episodic memories, also doesn't fully mature until our early twenties. While we might remember skills or particular items, we can't remember actual events from early childhood. In one study, six-month-olds who learned to press a lever to operate a train remembered how to do it for three weeks after they had last seen the toy. However, they couldn't remember events that had happened to them.

2. **Limited Language Skills.** Some experts believe that infants can't remember because they can't frame memories in linguistic terms, which prevents the memories from being organized and stored properly. While we don't need language to form memories, it helps us to rehearse them, both aloud to other people and in our heads. The suggestion is that memories can be formed, but can't be maintained.

One study interviewed people who had been to the hospital for an injury when they were toddlers. The infants aged over 26 months, who were able to speak at the time, remembered the incident up to five years later, while those under 26 months, who could not talk at the time, recalled nothing.

3. **No Sense of Self.** Some believe that infants need to develop a sense of self before they can remember things that happened to them. In one study, infants who could recognize themselves in a mirror had far better memory recall of where they'd hidden a teddy bear than those who could not.

4. **No Retrieval Cues.** Some experts think that infants have no trouble forming memories; they just can't recall them later in life. The theory is that because our perspective has changed so much since our early childhood, there are no retrieval cues to trigger a memory. They claim that even if we continue to live in the same house, everything looks so much different when we're older that nothing cues the memory. For example, a chair that once looked enormous later seems much smaller.

Despite the lack of memories that infants may have, it is universally accepted by psychologists that the accumulation of events does nevertheless have a lasting and powerful influence in shaping their personalities as adults.

Why Do Many Prices End in Ninety– Nine Cents?

A widely used practice among retailers in many parts of the world is to market goods so that the prices end in ninety-nine cents. This is a phenomenon sometimes known as "the nine fixation" and is thought to have begun in the late 19th century.

Goods are priced this way for a number of reasons, the predominant one of which is that people instinctively round the price down to the leading digit, so a price of $10.99 will be viewed as $10, which might persuade people to purchase as they subconsciously think they're getting a bargain. It also gives the impression that the retailer has discounted the price from the next rounded number. Psychologists claim that another reason for people to be seduced by this kind of marketing is that they may view the shopping experience more favorably if they receive change. By ending a price with ninety-nine cents, the retailer therefore gives the person the smallest amount of change possible, again maximizing profits.

Another possible reason for this kind of marketing is that people find the look of a combination of nines appealing. The aesthetic appeal of a $99.99 price tag, for example, might therefore make a person more inclined to purchase it.

It is also thought that the practice of such pricing actually started as a means of ensuring that cashiers had to open the cash register to give change, which made it more difficult for them simply to steal the money that had been given to them. Another, more compelling, explanation is that it allows the use of gimmicks such as advertising goods as being "under $100." By making the item $99.99, the retailer is true to his word and might succeed in luring the customer into the store where other items might then be purchased.

Some claim, however, that this method does not work because nine is a larger number than one and $99.99 has more digits than $100, and so seems more expensive. It can also prove counterproductive by causing confusion and annoyance among consumers, who might feel that they are being duped.

Does Alcohol Really Kill Brain Cells?

How many times do you hear it: "Don't drink too much alcohol; it'll kill your brain cells"? There is clear evidence that alcohol does do something to the brain. After a few drinks, people will slur their words, stumble when they walk, and experience memory loss. But have brain cells actually been killed, or is there another way to explain these debilitating symptoms?

Alcohol does not kill brain cells, but it does affect the brain. When it reaches the brain, alcohol inhibits the dendrites, the branching connections at the ends of neurons that send and receive messages between brain cells. This results in poor communication between the cells, causing cognitive and motor problems.

However, the brain has billions of neurons and dendrites, and research has shown that dendrite damage is reversible. Even in alcoholics, once drinking is stopped for a period of time, the dendrites repair and the ability of the brain cells to communicate is restored. Most significant, long-term alcohol-related disabilities are actually caused by malnutrition or a deficiency in vitamins.

Another side effect of excessive drinking is that alcohol inhibits the growth of new brain cells. But research on rats has shown that once the alcohol intake is stopped, even more brain cells are produced to compensate.

So, while alcohol can impair your brain, the effects are generally temporary and reversible. In fact, a number of studies have shown that drinking moderate amounts actually improves brain function and is associated with a reduced risk of dementia. It has been found that those who drink moderately on a regular basis have a reduced chance of becoming mentally ill later in life compared to those who don't drink. One study from 2001, conducted at the Catholic University of the Sacred Heart in Italy, found there was a 19 percent chance of mental impairment for people over 65 who were moderate drinkers, as opposed to a 29 percent chance among nondrinkers.

Why Do Gazelles Periodically Leap in the Air When Being Chased by Predators?

Watch an animal documentary set in Africa, and you will often see gazelles springing in the air if they are being chased by a predator. They tend to lift all four feet off the ground simultaneously, holding them in a stiff position while arching their back and pointing their head downward. Such a practice makes the gazelle more visible and uses up valuable time and energy when it could be getting farther away from the danger. This has led scientists to question why they do it—there must be a benefit.

A number of explanations have been proposed for this irregular quadruped behavior known as "stotting."

Some claim that it aids in the escape, and that the gazelle is jumping over obstacles. Others say it is used to get up high to detect predators, or that it is an alarm signal to other members of the herd. Still others say that it is a fitness display to potential mates. None of these theories is likely. Stotting usually takes place during an attack, when the predator has been seen and the entire herd is running for its life. There are three more realistic theories.

It confuses the predator. If a number of gazelles start stotting, a pursuing predator might have difficulty picking out an individual to chase. One study on stotting found that when hunting, wild dogs were, in fact, less likely to kill a gazelle when pursuing a herd in which more individuals stotted.

It is a predator detection signal. Stotting might be the gazelle's way of telling the predator that it has been seen and has lost the advantage of surprise, thereby discouraging it from pursuing the gazelle. This would benefit both animals, saving the gazelle from fleeing and saving the predator from wasting time stalking. Evidence has shown that cheetahs are more likely to abandon a hunt when a gazelle stots from the outset.

It is an honest signal of fitness. Gazelles might stot to indicate to the predator that the gazelle is fit and is not worth chasing. The gazelle is effectively saying that it is so fit and fast that it can escape even if it slows itself down by stotting. This theory is widely accepted, and gazelles that stot for a longer proportion of time in a chase have been found to be less likely to be killed by wild dogs.

❓ Does Sitting Close to the TV or Reading in Poor Light Ruin Your Eyes?

Parents are often heard warning their children about the dangers of sitting too close to the television or reading in low light, which have both been held as causes of ruining a person's eyesight.

The accusation with which the television is charged might have arisen because of the excessive X-rays that television sets emitted before the 1960s, but there is no medical evidence to suggest that sitting close to a modern set causes any damage to the eyes. Ophthalmology specialists maintain that the eyes of children can focus easily at very short distances without being strained, the only potential side effect being temporary eye fatigue. The same is true for prolonged exposure to computer monitors, which causes the eyes to dry out and become tired because people blink less while looking at them. However, further research is being conducted in this area.

Similarly, reading in dim light or watching television in the dark has no long-term effect on a person's vision. Again, adequate light merely reduces the likelihood that a person's eyes will become fatigued.

Some studies suggest that people who are introduced to modern technology from other cultures do experience a high degree of myopia, or nearsightedness. These studies are not conclusive, however, and many believe that any detrimental effects to eyesight are more likely to be as a result of a change in diet.

❓ Why Do Police Officers Hold Flashlights with an Overhand Grip?

In any cop movie or television show, the police officers always hold their flashlights in an overhand, or ice pick, grip. Nobody else ever seems to hold flashlights in this way, so why do the police?

The main reason is that by holding the light in this position, it can more easily be used as a defensive weapon. In the dark, an attack on the officer is likely to be unexpected, so the metal flashlight can be used to strike down on an attacker with force. If it were carried the other way, it would have to be raised and then lowered to hit someone. This would take up valuable time.

Holding it in this way can also act as a defensive device. With the light up high and away from the body, the idea is that the officer will disorient any attacker, who will tend to shoot at the light and miss the officer's body. Most people also tend to shoot high of a target; when they pull the trigger they jerk it, and the gun lifts, as well. This makes it more likely that any bullet would pass over the officer. If the light were held down low, the officer's body would be directly behind the light source and would be more likely to be hit by a bullet.

It is also more effective if an officer is looking into a car. With an underhanded grip, the officer would have to bend down to see. With an overhanded grip, it is far less awkward.

Another major advantage of the ice pick grip is that when cops in the movies hold a flashlight that way, it looks cool. And real-life police officers watch cop shows just like the rest of us.

❓ Do Vegetarians Live Longer?

Only a couple of decades ago, many people had not even met a vegetarian, but the number of Americans who are turning away from meat is rising steadily. There are a variety of reasons for this increase, such as ethics, religion, and health concerns. But does this popular new way of life actually make people live longer?

Much research over the years has linked eating red meat with a number of health risks including cardiovascular disease, stroke, diabetes, and certain cancers. Vegetarianism has been found to reduce these risks. One 2013 study that followed 96,000 Seventh-Day Adventists (whose religion advocates a vegetarian diet) showed a 12 percent lower risk of death than meat-eaters, and an increased average lifespan of six to nine years.

In 2012, a team led by T. Huang of Zhejiang University in Hangzhou, China, conducted a meta-analysis, which combined the data from multiple studies on vegetarianism. The team concluded that the risk of cancer in vegetarians was 18 percent lower, and the risk of death from heart disease 29 percent lower.

But is it all as simple as that? Many experts say it's not and claim that the statistics are skewed. On average, vegetarians are health-conscious people. They are less likely to smoke, drink alcohol, or be overweight, and more likely to exercise and be married. These are all factors that tend to contribute to a longer life, suggesting that factors other than an abstinence from meat may be the reason vegetarians live longer.

A 2003 article, "Mortality in British Vegetarians," written by a group led by Tim Key of the University of Oxford's Cancer Epidemiology Unit, drew similar conclusions, stating: "British vegetarians have low mortality compared with the general population. Their death rates are similar to those of comparable non-vegetarians, suggesting that much of this benefit may be attributed to non-dietary lifestyle factors such as a low prevalence of smoking and a generally high socioeconomic status, or to aspects of the diet other than the avoidance of meat and fish."

While there is still some debate on the topic, it seems that while vegetarians do generally live longer, their avoidance of meat is not the reason. And until the issue is resolved definitively, why live with regret and resist that big, juicy steak? As 103-year-old English vegetarian Roy Hobbs said in 2015, "It wasn't worth it."

Why Is There No Cure for the Common Cold?

The common cold is a mild viral disease that infects the nose, throat, and respiratory system. It generally results in nasal congestion, sneezing, coughing, and breathing difficulties.

The cold is the most common disease from which humans suffer, with most people getting at least one or two colds every year. As a group, it is estimated that Americans experience about one billion colds every year, which has a marked effect on the economy. Given that medical science has eradicated smallpox and polio, created vaccines for measles and mumps, and extended average life expectancy, people often rightly ask, "Why can't we cure the common cold?"

A cold is a general term for over two hundred viruses that can infect the body. The most common are the rhinoviruses, and even they have over a hundred strains. The viruses enter the cells in the nose, where they multiply and rapidly mutate in the human host to form new viruses.

The number and nature of these viruses make vaccination impractical.

Curing the cold would necessitate creating a single vaccine that would be effective for more than two hundred viruses, as a generalized rhinovirus vaccine would not protect against other types of viruses. Even creating a rhinovirus vaccine would be difficult, as there are usually up to thirty types of that virus circulating at any time, and only around 10 percent of those will be present the following year. Health officials are unable to predict which virus types will be prevalent each year. And because of the mutative abilities of the cold viruses, even if a vaccine could be created, it likely would no longer be useful by the time it was developed.

Only humans show cold-like symptoms, which rules out animal testing. And to test humans, a rhinovirus would have to be found that the subjects had not already been exposed to, which would be an almost impossible task.

The likely end result of all this is that when science has cured every other disease and we're all living until we're three hundred, the common cold will be just as common as it is today.

Is Baldness in Men a Sign of Virility?

Have you ever found that when you mention a lack of hair to a bald man, he'll reply, "It's a sign of virility"? The apparent link is testosterone. Bald men think that excess levels of testosterone lead to baldness, and as testosterone is the male hormone responsible for masculinity and sex drive, they are therefore more virile as well.

The association of baldness with virility has been around for millennia. Hippocrates and Aristotle noticed the link between eunuchs (people who had been castrated) and their lack of hair loss. James B. Hamilton, an anatomy graduate from Yale University in the 1930s, also studied the topic and noticed that men who had been castrated typically retained their hair.

While testosterone does cause baldness, it's not about the quantity circulating in the bloodstream, but rather how the testosterone signal is received in the hair follicle. And this comes down to genetics.

Male-pattern balding is caused by an enzyme called 5-alpha reductase, which converts testosterone into dihydrotestosterone (DHT). The DHT binds to receptor sites on the cells of hair follicles to cause specific changes. It inhibits hair growth, whereby healthy hair follicles start producing thinner and more brittle shafts of hair and can even die out. Bald men are genetically predisposed to be more sensitive to DHT. It's not the amount of testosterone present that causes baldness; it's the fact that testosterone converts to DHT. Men with low levels of testosterone can go bald, as long as there is some testosterone.

But perhaps there's hope yet. Are bald men more virile anyway?

No. A balding British dermatologist named John Burton studied the correlation between baldness and virility in 1979. In his study of 48 men aged between 35 and 64, he found that typical markers of masculinity such as hair density on the body, testosterone levels, and muscle and bone thickness showed no relationship to baldness whatsoever. All later studies have come to the same conclusion.

This is bad news for the follically challenged men out there, but don't worry too much; you still have your beards.

The chin follicles are not affected by DHT, so your beards will never fall out.

❓ Why Do You Often See a Single Shoe Lying on the Side of the Road?

Known as "the one shoe phenomenon," it is uncanny how often you see a lone boot or shoe lying on the side of the road. And the most puzzling thing is that the shoe is normally in a very noticeable place, like the middle of a busy intersection. Why does this happen? Where is the other shoe?

There are a number of hypotheses about why this happens with footwear more than other types of clothing, and why it happens at all.

Shoes, particularly leather ones, are more sturdily made than other types of clothing, so they will last a long time after being abandoned outside. Shoes are far easier to remove than other clothing, and their absence does not leave the wearer as embarrassingly exposed as does removing a shirt or a pair of pants. Shoes are also the easiest piece of clothing to throw.

By why are they out there in the first place?

Officials at both the United States Department of Transportation and the National Highway Traffic Safety Administration are aware of the presence of abandoned shoes, but they have not offered an explanation. Here are a few possible theories.

- They fall out of garbage trucks.
- They are one of a pair of shoes cut away from the back bumper of a newlywed's car.
- They come loose when people dangle their feet from car windows.

- Both shoes are abandoned but become separated when one rolls away.
- Dogs take one shoe, and, tired of gnawing on it, leave it by the road.

While some shoe abandonment is probably accidental and caused by one of the above reasons, the most likely explanation is that the shoe has been thrown there on purpose.

The most cogent theory is that they're thrown out of school buses or cars during fights or as practical jokes. There is a certain thrill in throwing an object from a moving vehicle, and shoes make useful projectiles, as they can be thrown a distance from the car to avoid detection from authorities. And the more noticeable the placement of the shoe, the more satisfying the act.

Given that many people now discuss the strange concept of the lone abandoned shoe when they see one, the phenomenon has become self-perpetuating, and it's likely that an even higher percentage of shoes will suffer this ignominious fate.

What Is the Difference between Monkeys and Apes?

Apes and monkeys are often confused, and the terms are sometimes used synonymously. However, while both are primates, they are completely different classes of animals.

The confusion arises because of the similarities in appearance of the two groups. While they're often called monkeys, chimpanzees and gibbons are actually apes, as are gorillas and orangutans. Similarly, monkeys are often wrongly classed as apes, some even having the word "ape" in their name.

There are many species of monkeys, and they vary considerably in size and appearance. Some live in trees and some on the ground, and their diets range from insects to fruit and leaves. Most monkeys have tails while apes do not.

Apes, meanwhile, have more teeth than monkeys do and eat both meat and vegetation. They also have more mobile shoulder joints and arms for brachiating (i.e., swinging through trees), which most monkeys are unable to do. However, apes' spines aren't as mobile as those of monkeys, who tend to run along tree branches and have the skeletal shape of cats and dogs. Both animals have forward-facing eyes.

In evolutionary terms, apes are far closer to humans than monkeys are. They possess the same basic body structure, exhibit similar behavioral patterns, and have developed complex social cultures. Apes are also capable of using tools and are far more intelligent than monkeys, even demonstrating impressive language and learning capabilities. Genetically speaking, chimpanzees are the closest living relatives to humans.

Capuchin monkey   *Chimpanzee (ape)*

🟰 Do Plants Feel Pain?

The question as to whether plants feel pain has been hotly debated for years. One of the reasons for this is the difference between plant cognition and plant perception.

Plant perception is the ability of plants to sense and respond to the environment. There is no doubt that plants do possess this ability, to varying degrees. Plants react to light, moisture, insects, temperature, and many other factors. Many plants use molecular responses and chemical communications to protect themselves. In some cases, they do this by emitting a poison to ward off insects, or a chemical to attract bees. Wounded tomatoes produce a particular odor as an alarm signal to neighboring plants, which allows them to produce different chemicals in defense against the attacking insects. Sunflowers turn toward the sun, the mimosa plant makes its leaves turn down if they are touched, and the Venus flytrap snaps shut to kill insects that land on it.

A 1997 study on plant perception conducted at the Institute for Applied Physics at the University of Bonn in Germany shed even more light on the matter. Using a laser-powered microphone, the researchers found that sound waves are produced by gases that plants release when they are cut or injured. These gases, they said, are the equivalent of us crying out in pain.

While these examples of plant sophistication indicate that plants may be able to experience pain, many scientists assert that plant perception is very distinct from plant cognition. Because a plant does not have a brain, they maintain that no feelings of pain can be registered. Plants do not possess a nervous system and, without one, plants have neither a mechanism for feeling pain, nor the ability to experience emotions such as suffering. It is purely chemistry that dictates plant behaviors and reactions, similar to how an involuntary chemical reaction causes human skin to increase melanin production when it is exposed to sunlight.

Because there is no evidence for the presence of neurons in plants, the majority of scientists consider the idea of plant cognition to be unfounded and absurd.

So, while plants can definitely communicate, it is unlikely that they can feel pain in the way we do. That said, we may never know for sure, and a 2014 study at the University of Missouri, Columbia, found something that very few vegetarians will find appetizing: plants are able to register and react to the sounds of insects chewing them. If that's true, perhaps it's best to avoid any eye contact with the lettuce on your plate.

Why Do Roosters Crow?

To the bane of many country dwellers, roosters are often heard crowing in the early hours of the morning. The sound they make is generally written as "cock-a-doodle-doo." It is one of the most common sounds of rural life. Many people believe that roosters crow as the sun rises as an announcement of the dawn of a new day. But roosters often crow before the sun rises. It is thought that they crow on a daily cycle, and the internal "body clock" of the rooster anticipates the dawn and wakes the rooster for crowing. If the rooster's body clock wakes him early, crowing will start before dawn.

Some believe that a rooster crows to attract hens, and because this may also attract predators, the safest time to crow is before the sun is very high in the sky. Others think a rooster crows to indicate that he has found some food that is worthy of note, or to keep the flock together if any chickens venture out of sight. Others believe that a rooster crows when it is in high spirits.

Most ornithologists now agree that the main purpose of the call is to establish and mark out the rooster's territory. Before they were domesticated, roosters traveled with flocks of hens and would claim areas for their territory, warding off competing roosters with a powerful crow. The reason roosters tend to crow from a prominent vantage point, such as a fence post, is to make themselves clearly visible to their competitors and to ensure that the noise travels farther. Ornithologists say that the reason most roosters crow early in the morning is that, like other birds, it is when they are most active. The morning is the start of a new day, and the rooster is crowing to reaffirm his territory to outsiders.

But roosters are known to crow at any time of the day or night. This may be prompted by a foreign noise that the rooster interprets as a challenge and so feels the need to announce his territory. Once one rooster starts crowing, it tends to stimulate others to follow suit. The most effective way to reduce or stop a rooster from crowing is castration. This procedure leaves the rooster with fewer male hormones and a similarly decreased inclination to defend his territory.

Does a Goldfish's Memory Really Only Last a Few Seconds?

It is a popular belief that a goldfish has a virtually nonexistent memory span, and every lap of the fishbowl is like seeing the world for the first time. It turns out that this is not true—far from it, in fact.

Goldfish are actually very intelligent creatures and have excellent memories. They can be trained to respond to different colors of light and types of music, push levers to receive food, and find their way around mazes. They can even tell the time (sort of). Scientists at the University of St. Andrews in Scotland claim that goldfish are at least as intelligent as rats.

These harmless little fish have been shown to be able to recognize their owners and don't consider them a threat, even if touched by them. They can respond to the appearance and voice of their owners. Yet around strangers, the fish will often hide.

A number of experiments have been conducted to test their intelligence. In one, the fish had to learn to escape a net through a small hole. They succeeded after about five trials,

and after a gap of a year, they were able to remember the exact escape route straightaway.

In another experiment, researchers trained goldfish to associate a certain sound with feeding time. The fish were then released into deeper waters. Five months later, the same sound was broadcast over a loudspeaker and the fish returned to their original feeding place.

In another study, researchers at Plymouth University in England trained goldfish to nudge a lever to get food. When the lever was pressed, food was dispensed. The lever was then set so that food would only be given at the same time every day, for one hour. The fish quickly learned to only press the lever at the correct time, and they ignored it for the rest of the day.

These studies show just how intelligent these animals really are, so the next time someone tells you that you have a memory like a goldfish, take it as a compliment.

❓ How Did the Strange Scoring System in Tennis Come About?

Presented with the sequence 15-0, 15-30, 30-30, 40-30—not even Einstein would have been able to calculate the next set of numbers in that progression. And then they say "love" for 0. How *did* the arcane tennis scoring system originate?

One theory of the origin of "love" is that the players have love for each other when neither has yet scored. Another theory is that it derives from a Dutch expression meaning something done for praise, with no money at stake.

These two explanations are unlikely, however, and most tennis historians believe that it comes from the French word *l'oeuf*, meaning the egg, because of an egg's resemblance to the number zero. Over the years, the pronunciation of the French word was altered until it became "love."

Three possibilities explain the use of 15, 30, and 40 in tennis. Nobody knows which is correct, and all seem equally meritorious.

It is thought that clock faces might have been used on the courts to keep score, with a quarter move of the hand to indicate the scores of 15, 30, and 45. When the hand reached 60, the game had been won. However, to ensure that the game could not be won by only one point, the idea of *deuce* was introduced, meaning two, or that both players were equal. To make the score stay within the clock face's 60, the 45 was changed to 40. This allowed another two points to be easily divided. If both players were at 40, or deuce, the next score moved the player to 50 (now "advantage"), and another point took the player to 60 to win the game. Opponents of this theory say that clocks in medieval times, when the scoring system was developed, only recorded the hours from 1 to 12 and did not have minute hands.

A similar theory involves the use of a circle. Medieval Europeans were interested in astronomy and geometry. In early records of the game in France, sets were played to four or six games. A sextant, being one-sixth of a circle, was 60 degrees, so each point was worth 15 degrees, making a game 60 degrees. By winning six games, a player had completed a full circle of 360 degrees, and so had won the set. The 45 may have later been changed to 40 for the same reason outlined in the clock theory.

The final theory is that the scoring system came from the French game *jeu de paume*, a precursor to tennis that used the hand instead of a racket. This game was very popular before the French Revolution, with more than a thousand courts in Paris alone. The court was 90 feet long, 45 feet on each side of the net. Upon scoring, the server got to move up 15 feet, then another 15 feet if another point was scored. As a third move of 15 feet would place the server at the net, 10 feet was the final move, giving the scores of 15, 30, and 40.

Does Sugar Make Kids Hyper?

Many parents will attest to the fact that a single bite of birthday cake will turn their polite and perfectly behaved angel into a maniacal demon who runs around the room terrorizing everyone and everything. Anyone who's been to a toddler's birthday party will probably agree that this hypothesis sounds reasonable, but does a small, sugary treat really lead to a hyperactive frenzy?

The research says no. Not at all.

Dr. Mark Wolraich, the chief of Developmental and Behavioral Pediatrics at the Oklahoma University Health Sciences Center, studied the effects of sugar on children in the 1990s. His 1994 study published in the *New England Journal of Medicine* found that sugar does not appear to affect behavior in children. Instead, he found that it was the parents' expectations of so-called sugar highs that colored the way they viewed the cause of their children's behavior. He said that children tended to be more hyperactive at birthday parties because they were excited, not because of the sugar they had eaten. Parents, however, have made the incorrect link.

Indeed, a 1994 study reported in the *Journal of Abnormal Child Psychology* found parents to be more likely to say their child was hyperactive even when the "sugar" fix was a placebo.

Half the mothers in the study were told their children had been given a sugary drink, and it was these mothers who rated their children as more hyperactive. These mothers were also more likely to criticize their children, thinking they were behaving badly because of the "sugar."

In another 1994 study published in the *New England Journal of Medicine*, three sets of children were given three different diets for three weeks. One diet was high in sugar, one high in a noncaloric sweetener, and one with no sweetener. It was found that there were no significant differences among the three groups of children, leading to the conclusion that sugar did not have an impact on the intelligence or behavior of children.

In 1995, Dr. Mark Wolraich also conducted a review of sixteen studies done on the topic. The statistician who looked at the results said that "he had never had such consistently negative results," meaning that sugar did not correlate to hyperactivity.

So, how did the sugar-high myth arise? The misconception comes from the idea that increased blood sugar levels translate into hyperactivity. It is true that someone with low blood-sugar levels can get an energy boost from sugar, but if the body needs that energy, it will use it, and if it doesn't, the sugar will be converted into fat for storage. In fact, sugar can have a soothing effect, temporarily increasing calming neurochemicals in the brain, such as serotonin.

So, should you give your child sugary drinks and food? While there are plenty of good reasons not to feed your children excess sugar, such as potential weight gain and dental deterioration, the fear of them turning into crazed sugar monsters who run around the house destroying everything in their path is not one of them.

Was Nostradamus Able to Predict the Future?

Michel de Nostredame, commonly known as Nostradamus, lived in France between 1503 and 1566. A well-educated man, he is famous for his book *Les Prophéties*, a compendium of various prophecies that take the form of rhymed four-lined poems called quatrains, grouped in sets of centuries. Nostradamus is said to have concocted his prophecies by entering a trancelike state of meditation.

Nostradamus

Many believed Nostradamus to possess supernatural powers, and he has been credited with predicting a large number of historical events; indeed, he became famous during his lifetime by supposedly predicting the death of King Henry II of France. People have translated from his writings some other predictions, including those of the atomic bomb, the Great Fire of London, the French Revolution, the discoveries of Louis Pasteur, and the atrocities perpetrated by Hitler's Third Reich.

One of Nostradamus's most famous predictions was that a great disaster would occur in July 1999—a disaster that, in fact, did not happen. In the typical style of his prophecies, it read: "In the year 1999 and seven months, / a great King of Terror will come from the sky. / He will bring back the great king Genghis Khan, / before and after Mars rules happily." It is also said by some that he predicted the 9/11 terrorist attacks in the prophecy that reads, "At forty-five degrees, the sky will burn. / Fire approaches the great new city. / Immediately a huge scattered flame leaps up, / When they want to have verification from the Normans." In fact, New York City is below the forty-first parallel; but as often happens with Nostradamus's prophecies, this quatrain was misquoted to make it more relevant to 9/11 and then circulated on the internet.

Skeptics claim that Nostradamus's prophecies are written in an intentionally ambiguous manner and are sufficiently vague as to be capable of being applied to many events, while the prophecies are further obscured by often being written in a mixture of languages. Critics also argue that the prophecies have always been interpreted with the benefit of hindsight in what is called "retroactive clairvoyance." None of the prophecies has been interpreted before a specific event.

Why Were Prehistoric Animals So Big?

While there were many small animals in prehistoric times, the land was dominated by oversized versions of our modern animals—giant snakes, giant sharks, giant birds, and really giant lizards. What was it about that era that made the animals so massive?

A number of environmental factors could account for their size.

In cold climates, a large frame could have assisted a warm-blooded animal in retaining heat, and in hot climates, a bigger mass could have helped insulate a cold-blooded animal and stopped it from overheating.

Higher oxygen content in the air and more space in which to live may have contributed to their size.

Some scientists believe that the size of plant-eating dinosaurs may have been caused by the tough and woody foliage they were eating. The animals needed a large digestive tract to allow more time for bacteria to break down the food, and this led to a larger animal overall.

All of these theories may have some validity, but the most common reason cited by experts is simple: time. Because of evolution, animals tend to get larger over time, and these animals had millions of years to grow. This is known as Cope's rule, named after the 19th-century paleontologist Edward Cope. Being larger than other animals of a species tends to offer an evolutionary advantage, allowing an animal to fight for territory, food, and mates, as well as making them less vulnerable to predation. Natural selection drives many animals to become larger over time.

After the dinosaurs were wiped out, smaller animals took their place, growing larger over time to turn into impressive beasts like the woolly mammoth and saber-toothed tiger. They lived during the last ice age, which lasted between 2.6 million and 12,000 years ago. Each time a set of animals is devastated, it takes millions of years for the next generation to grow big again. The last major extinction took place around 12,000 years ago, which is not nearly enough time for animals to grow massive again. But, given enough time, they probably will.

Which makes you wonder just how big the blue whale will end up, as it is the largest animal ever to have existed.

Is Using a Cell Phone at a Gas Station Actually Dangerous?

If you dare to use your cell phone while filling up at a gas station, other motorists will start jumping up and down and the manager will probably come running out to stop you. There are warnings posted at every station about not using cell phones, and even cell phone manuals state not to use them at gas stations. Using a cell phone at a gas station is obviously extremely dangerous, right?

No, not at all.

Rumors have circulated for years suggesting that using a cell phone in the presence of fuel vapors is highly dangerous. The theory is that an electrical spark from the phone will ignite the vapors and cause a fire or explosion. As a result of these rumors, and out of an abundance of caution, the gas stations have posted the warnings. But the risk is very, very low—to the point of being minute.

It is theoretically possible to cause a fire with a cell phone. Though there is easily enough energy in the phone's battery to produce a spark to ignite a fire, a phone doesn't produce a spark, and even if the battery did, the spark would likely be too small and would be contained within the phone casing anyway. The lithium battery could also potentially explode while it is charging if the internal circuitry is faulty, but this is very unlikely as well, and you wouldn't normally be talking on a charging phone while pumping gas.

Then there's the electrical field that your cell phone produces. The field has been measured at two to five volts per meter, which has never been known to set off a fire. Nearby cell phone towers create a far greater electrical field and would actually be much more likely to start a fire at a gas station.

So, has a cell phone ever set off a fire at a gas station? No. The Australian Transport Safety Bureau assessed 243 gas station fires worldwide over an eleven-year period, and none was caused by cell phones.

Even the United States government agrees that the risks are low. The Federal Communications Commission has concluded that the potential threat is remote, while the Cellular Telecommunications Industry Association has said that there is no evidence at all that a cell phone has caused an explosion at a gas station anywhere in the world. A representative from the American Petroleum Institute reiterated this fact, saying, "We have not found a cell phone responsible for any fire since the beginning of mankind."

So, what's causing the gas station fires? Static electricity, mostly. If a person wearing synthetic clothes in dry weather slides across a fabric car seat, they can build up a significant static charge. If the earthing wire of the pump hose is broken, a visible spark can discharge when the metal nozzle is touched to the metal of the car's tank, which is enough to ignite the gas vapors and start a fire.

But in the end, the cell phone myth is just that—endless chatter. Just make sure it doesn't generate too much static.

Why Do People Have Eyebrows?

As humans evolved, we lost most of the thick hair that once covered our bodies. But why did we keep that little bit over the eyes, and what purpose does it serve? It might amaze you to discover that those innocent strips of hair could well be the reason we are here today.

Eyebrows assisted greatly in the survival of early humans. Apart from deflecting debris and shielding the eyes from the sun, they rain and sweat out of our eyes. The arch shape diverts the moisture to the side of the face, keeping the eyes dry so that our vision remains clear. This would have helped our ancestors find shelter in the rain, and it would have helped them escape predators. Running from an attack would likely produce sweat, and if sweat got in the eyes, it would have caused irritation, impaired vision, and made it more difficult to escape. Given this survival advantage, natural selection would have picked those who had eyebrows.

Some scientists also suggest that eyebrows, combined with eyelashes, served as eyespots, creating the illusion that a person's eyes were open even when they were asleep. Nighttime predators such as big cats are far less likely to attack prey if they think the prey is watching them. This also would have provided a distinct survival advantage to our ancestors.

Another reason eyebrows were retained is that they play a significant psychological role. They are one of our most expressive facial features and are essential for nonverbal communication. The different positions and movements of eyebrows are key to signaling changes in mood, expressing surprise, happiness, and anger. This was important from an evolutionary perspective, as early humans' survival hinged on strong-functioning and close-knit tribes.

Eyebrows are also a very distinctive aspect of human appearance and act as identification cards. They stand out from the forehead and can be clearly seen from a distance. This would have been helpful for distinguishing between friend and enemy on the open plains. In fact, experiments have shown that we can recognize a familiar face more easily when the eyes are obscured than when the eyebrows are. This was shown in a 2002 study published by students at the Massachusetts Institute of Technology. In 60 percent of all trials, people were able to successfully recognize photos of celebrities with their eyes edited out, compared with a 46 percent success rate when the eyebrows were removed.

Do Skunks Think Skunks Stink?

If you've ever seen the *Looney Tunes* cartoon character, Pepé Le Pew, you may well have the view that skunks relish their own stench, never allowing it to reduce their self-esteem. But is there any truth to this Warner Bros. depiction, or do skunks, too, find their odor offensive?

There are eleven species of skunks, but it's not the skunk itself that smells. Rather, it's what they spray as a defense from predators such as foxes, badgers, and wolves. By using an oil gland adjacent to their anus, skunks shoot a plume of chemicals called thiols. These thiols are sulfur compounds that can cause headaches and burning in the eyes. Skunks can aim with surprising force and can accurately hit a target up to 10 feet away. But the worst part about their spray is the smell, which can linger on a victim for weeks. Sometimes described as a combination of garlic, rotten eggs, and burnt rubber, the smell acts as a significant deterrent to predators, causing even large bears to keep their distance.

But what about other skunks? According to Dr. Jerry Dragoo, the head of the Dragoo Institute for the Betterment of Skunks and Skunk Reputations, skunks do not find their odor pleasant at all. Skunks have a very strong sense of smell and find the odor offensive. If a skunk is hit by the spray, it will rub its face in the dirt or try to groom itself to remove the irritant. Out of courtesy, however, skunks rarely spray each other, except during mating season. In the 2016 *Mental Floss* article, "Do Skunks Know They Stink?" Dragoo said, "As for their own scent, when skunks spray, they rarely get any on themselves, but it does happen. Though they can tolerate their own smell, they do not appreciate getting it in the face and eyes."

For this reason and the fact that after five uses they have to wait about ten days to replenish their stocks, skunks use their spray reluctantly and will usually resort to hissing, foot-stamping, and threatening postures before unleashing the stench. But when they do, look out—no animal, including a skunk, wants to be hit.

So, as it turns out, the Warner Bros. cartoons may not be as scientifically accurate as many people once thought.

Why Does Traffic Jam for No Apparent Reason?

Everyone has experienced the frustration of a "phantom traffic jam." The traffic just seems to stop for no apparent reason, and by the time you're moving freely again, you cannot see what might have caused it—there is no accident, no roadwork, no police interference. So, why do these jams happen?

If there are enough cars on a highway, any minor disruption to the flow of traffic can trigger a chain reaction. All it takes is for one car to brake unexpectedly. A driver might get too close to the car in front, look at the scenery and lose concentration, change lanes in front of another car, or slow down because of a bump in the road. The driver then brakes slightly, forcing the unsuspecting drivers behind to react with their own brakes so they can stay at a safe distance. A ripple effect occurs and the braking amplifies backward. It's like a shock wave that becomes more pronounced as it works its way back until a traffic jam is produced.

❓ Why Do We Have Leap Years?

A leap year, also known as an intercalary year, occurs about every four years to synchronize the calendar year with the solar year. Pretty simple, right? Sort of.

The solar year is the length of time it takes the earth to complete one orbit of the sun, which is approximately 365.2425 days. As the calendar year is only 365 days, an extra day is added to February, the shortest month, about every four years. If this variance weren't adjusted for, we would lose almost six hours from each calendar year, which, after a hundred years, would amount to twenty-four days.

The four-year model was adopted in the Julian calendar, introduced by Julius Caesar in 45 BC. However, the length of a solar year is slightly less than 365¼ days—less by eleven minutes. To compensate for this discrepancy, Pope Gregory XIII introduced the Gregorian calendar in 1582. This is the calendar we currently use, and it omits a leap year three times every four hundred years. A century year is not a leap year unless it is divisible by 400—so 1700, 1800, and 1900 were not leap years, but 1600 and 2000 were. This more closely equates the calendar and solar years, and using this method, it will take more than three thousand years for the calendar year to gain one extra day.

The term "leap year" comes from the fact that a fixed date in the calendar advances one day of the week each year. That is, if your birthday was on a Tuesday this year, it'll be on a Wednesday next year. But in the 12 months following a leap day (from March 1 to February 28), a date will advance by two days, thus "leaping" over a day.

The chance of being born on a leap day is about 1 in 1,500, and there are various traditions associated with leap years. In Britain, it is said that women can only propose marriage in leap years, while in Greece, marriage in a leap year is considered unlucky.

Leap days have other costs and benefits. If you're an employee being paid a salary and it falls mid-week, it's an extra day you have to work for no money. Bad for you, good for your boss. If your birthday falls on a leap day, you should only get presents every four years, but then you would technically age four times more slowly than the rest of us.

Why Can't You Tickle Yourself?

This is a question that has bedeviled philosophers as far back as Aristotle.

Scientists believe that when we are tickled, our bodies panic and enter a defensive state. This reaction is thought to have developed in our early ancestors in response to the attack of certain types of predators, such as spiders, whose progress across the skin the act of tickling is said to mimic. In modern times, because we know there is no danger, our reaction to being tickled is to laugh, either because we're not prepared to be tickled, and it takes us by surprise, or because of the anticipation of being tickled and not knowing exactly when or where it will occur.

The area of the brain that deals with coordination and sensory signals when we move is the cerebellum. It is here that our brain determines what to expect when the body performs movements and where it differentiates between expected and unexpected sensations. Typically, the cerebellum ignores expected sensations caused by the body's own movements while being very sensitive to unexpected ones. One example of this in action is that people don't notice their tongue movements when they talk or eat. Similarly, when we try to tickle ourselves, we are in control of the movement; the element of surprise is lost, and our brain predicts where we're going to touch ourselves and prepares for this. There is no natural internal tension or panic and no corresponding reaction like that which occurs when others tickle us. These "self-awareness signals" are delivered by the brain in a split second—too fast for us to fool ourselves, therefore preventing us from tickling ourselves.

Charles Darwin believed that tickling was a form of social interaction, making people laugh through the anticipation of pleasure. He postulated that for tickling to be effective, the recipient must not be aware of the exact point of contact, which is why people are unable to tickle themselves.

It is thought that some people with schizophrenic disorders, who at times suffer from delusions and have difficulty distinguishing between self-generated and external touch, may be able to tickle themselves if they are unable to predict the precise point of contact.

If Only Female Mosquitoes Bite, What Do the Males Eat?

You walk outside on a hot summer's night and are immediately attacked by a swarm of mosquitoes. Are they really all females? And if they are, what are the males eating?

Yes, they're all females. Only female mosquitoes bite. But blood is not their main food source.

Mosquitoes rely on sugar as their main source of energy, and both males and females feed on plant nectar, mainly from flowers. They use this nectar as fuel to fly and survive, and they replenish it on a daily basis. Mosquitoes actually help pollinate many plant species.

Female mosquitoes don't require blood for survival, but they need it to obtain protein and iron to develop fertile eggs. Nectar lacks these ingredients, so mosquitoes look toward us to get it.

Once the female has obtained some blood, fertilization by the male will occur. Then, she'll rest for a couple of days before laying her eggs.

Those eggs will hatch, the next generation of female mosquitoes will then suck more blood, and the whole process perpetuates, with us as the hapless accessories.

Why Do Doctors Have Such Messy Handwriting?

We've all experienced it. You go to the doctor, who gives you a prescription, and when you try to read it, it's completely illegible and looks like something a toddler might have produced. How could anyone possibly make it through medical school with such horrendous handwriting? And how does the pharmacist manage to read it?

The leading theory behind their extraordinary handwriting is that they're in a hurry, both physically and mentally. Doctors generally have a large workload, and as the number of their patients increases, the quality of their handwriting deteriorates. Before computers became common, doctors were legally required to handwrite a lot of notes documenting the symptoms and treatment for each patient. The time pressure associated with these notes led to messy writing.

Doctors may realize that they are likely the only ones who will have to read their penmanship. Most of the time it will just be the doctor referring to the notes, which will end up filed away, never to see the light of day again. What's the point in writing neatly in these circumstances?

And then there's the more cynical theory. The doctors could hold the belief that they are supposed to have bad handwriting, and so write that way on purpose.

But how do the pharmacists cope? A doctor's handwriting is usually decipherable by others in the profession because they are familiar with the medical terms and drug names, and so are able to put them into context. They are also more experienced in reading terrible writing, so have developed that skill.

But it's not all a big joke. Court juries are more likely to associate illegible handwriting with substandard medical care in malpractice suits.

Why Do People Say "Cheese" When Being Photographed?

"Say cheese!" is the simple instruction issued by photographers to elicit a smile from those being photographed, regardless of their age. It has become so commonplace that the word "say" is often omitted from the command, and most subjects don't even respond. They just know to smile at that point. But how did this bizarre directive come about?

Etymologists are unsure as to who coined the phrase, or if there is any link between the expression and the word cheese. It is generally thought that it was probably coined impromptu by a photographer, but nobody knows who or when. The word is useful for this purpose because the "ch" sound causes a person to open the lips while the "ee" sound pushes the cheeks outward, draws back the lips, and bares the teeth in a pose that resembles a smile.

The earliest recorded references to the saying are from the 1940s, when the phrase was popularized. In particular, the article "Need to Put on a Smile? Here's How: Say 'Cheese,'" from an October 1943 edition of the Texas newspaper *The Big Spring Daily Herald*, made this comment: "Now here's something worth knowing. It's a formula for smiling when you have your picture taken. It comes from former Ambassador Joseph E. Davies and is guaranteed to make you look pleasant no matter what you're thinking. Mr. Davies disclosed the formula while having his own picture taken on the set of *Mission to Moscow*. It's simple. Just say 'cheese,' it's an automatic smile. 'I learned that from a politician,' Mr. Davies chuckled."

It is thought that the politician referenced in the article was Franklin D. Roosevelt, who Davies served under, so we may well owe "say cheese" to none other than FDR. Whatever its origins, it was certainly an improvement on what was used in the late 19th century. At that time, a small, tightly shut mouth was considered beautiful, so there was a different, less jovial expression that was said to obtain the desired face: "Say prunes."

Does Lightning Ever Strike the Same Place Twice?

Everyone has heard the old saying "lightning never strikes the same place twice." Myth, or no myth?

Myth. Lightning can strike any location, any number of times.

When a cloud becomes electrically charged and the field of energy between the two ends of the cloud is strong enough, a discharge called a stepped leader starts from the cloud to the ground, zigzagging down in progressive steps. Once the stepped leader is close to the  ground, a "streamer" of the opposite charge shoots up from the ground or from something on the ground. This closes the circuit and triggers a rush of electricity in the form of a lightning bolt.

And lightning has no memory. If an object has been struck once, it is no less likely to be struck a second time. Tall objects such as skyscrapers, radio towers, or mountains are more likely to be struck repeatedly because their streamers narrow the gap between the ground and the cloud above, making them better targets.

The Eiffel Tower has been struck by lightning many times, and the shuttle launchpad at Cape Canaveral in Florida gets repeatedly hit, sometimes more than once during the same storm. The Empire State Building in New York City gets struck by lightning about twenty-five times each year.

That said, it's not just tall buildings that lightning strikes. It can strike low objects as well, even flat ground or people. And it can do so more than once.

If you don't believe that, you should talk to Roy Sullivan (if he were still alive, that is). Roy was a United States park ranger in Shenandoah National Park, Virginia. Between 1942 and 1977, he was struck by lightning on seven different occasions, surviving all of them, and earning him a place in the *Guinness Book of World Records*.

Why Do Firehouses Often Have Dalmatians?

Dalmatians have been depicted as firehouse dogs so often in movies and books that they're practically a stereotype. How did that come about?

The tradition of Dalmatians in firehouses dates back more than a century to a time when they once played a vital role. The English aristocrats of the early 1700s used the dogs to accompany their horse-drawn carriages. The dogs were very adept at keeping pace with the carriages over long distances and would defend the horses from other dogs or animals. They became a status symbol or badge of honor, and the more you had, the higher up the social ladder you appeared to be.

Because of their association with carriages, in the early times of firefighting, when horse-drawn carriages were driven to fires, Dalmatians were employed to run alongside. And they served a number of key purposes.

The dogs were kept in the firehouses, and when the alarm sounded, they would run out barking. This would alert bystanders to clear out of the way so that the carriage could easily exit. The dogs would then run alongside the carriage, scaring away anything that might spook the horses and barking to alert pedestrians to move out of the way. Once at the fire, the dogs provided comfort to the horses, who were generally afraid of fire, and stood guard at the wagon, ensuring that nobody stole the firefighters' belongings, equipment, or even the horses themselves.

Despite the fact that fire trucks are now used, many firehouses still keep Dalmatians and the tradition has been preserved. They have turned into firehouse mascots, particularly popular when firefighters go around teaching children about fire safety. And the dogs still protect the firefighters' possessions, but these days they ride inside the trucks instead of running alongside.

 ## How Does Aspirin Find the Pain?

Aspirin is probably the most well-known painkiller available. But how does it pinpoint the exact location of the pain?

Aspirin is a type of drug known as a COX-2 inhibitor. Damaged cells produce the COX-2 enzyme, which in turn produces prostaglandins, unsaturated fatty acids that the cells of the body secrete to cause pain and inflammation to highlight an area of injury. They also cause a damaged area to release fluid to create a protective cushion. This results in swelling.

Aspirin is a derivative of salicylic acid, which comes from the bark of willow and birch trees. Aspirin dissolves into the bloodstream, and, once at the site of any cell damage, binds to the COX-2 enzymes and blocks them from producing the pain-causing prostaglandins. As a result, inflammation is reduced and no more pain signals are sent to the brain.

Why Do Only Old Men Have Hairy Ears?

Hair is not the friend of the aging man. While the hair on his scalp thins and falls out, it springs up in new places, like the shoulders, back, nose, and ears. But why do formerly bare ears suddenly become hirsute?

Vellus hair is short, thin, barely noticeable hair that covers most of a person's body during childhood. As people age, some of the vellus hair changes. During and after puberty, this hair can transform into thicker, darker hair known as terminal hair. This happens to a greater extent in men than in women, and by the time some men are old, the soft and downy vellus hair on and in their ears changes into something you'd expect to see on a werewolf.

The cause of this transformation isn't fully understood.

The leading theory to explain the hairy ears is prolonged exposure to testosterone. While the testosterone levels in old men usually drop, it is thought that the hormone may have a cumulative effect, so that as a man ages, the hair follicles are exposed to a greater overall amount of testosterone, and this encourages the growth of long black hairs.

Scientists also believe that the hairy ears of older men could be related to the fact that they go bald on their heads. Male-pattern balding is caused by an enzyme called 5-alpha reductase, which converts testosterone into dihydrotestosterone (DHT). The DHT binds to receptor sites on the cells of the hair follicles to cause specific changes. On the head, these changes inhibit hair growth, while on the ears, they enhance it. The result: long, black, coarse ear hair. Supporting this theory is the fact that women rarely go bald, and they rarely have bushy ear hair either.

Whichever theory is correct, most experts agree that testosterone is responsible in some way for the hairy ears of old men. So, while many men want a lot of testosterone to make them manly, there's certainly a balance to be struck. Too much can make men appear a little more manly than they might like.

Can Police Dogs Really Sniff Out Drugs?

The German shepherd, Belgian Malinois, and Labrador retriever breeds possess an incredible sense of smell and strong hunting instincts. Coupled with their extensive training, these attributes make them excellent police sniffer dogs, highly driven to detect illicit substances. But just how good are they? What's their success rate?

Sniffer dogs undergo intensive training. It usually involves a white towel. After playing a game with the dog and the towel, the handler then rolls a bag of drugs inside it. This makes the dog associate the smell of the drugs with the game. The handler then hides the towel and the drugs and if the dog finds it, the handler uses the towel to play a game of tug-of-war with the dog. The dog soon comes to associate finding the drugs with a rewarding game. But, despite this training, some people remain skeptical. In 2011, the *Chicago Tribune* claimed that the dogs' responses are influenced by the biases and behaviors of their handlers. After examining three years of data for dogs used in roadside traffic stops, it was claimed that only 44 percent of the dogs' positive signals led to the discovery of drugs.

Another study, published by Lisa Lit in the journal *Animal Cognition* in 2011, also brings into question the effectiveness of sniffer dogs. Researchers placed packages inside a church and led the handlers to believe that certain packages contained drugs  when, in fact, none of them did. Despite there never being any drugs whatsoever placed in the church, 225 alerts were issued by the 18 handlers and their dogs, all of them incorrect. Indeed, drastically more false alarms occurred in places where red markers were positioned to indicate the presence of drugs to the handlers.

Dog behavioral experts believe these skewed statistics are the result of dogs relying on cues from their handlers, whether the cues are intentional or subconscious. Dogs have been shown to rely more heavily on human cues, such as eye contact, glances, and body orientation, than their own sight and smell when looking for food. A classic example is how a dog generally prefers to look for food in an empty bowl that a human is pointing to, instead of in a full bowl of food that it can see and smell.

With these studies in mind, can sniffer dogs really be trusted to detect drugs? Perhaps, but it seems the subjective opinion of the police dog handler might be just as influential as the dog's heightened sense of smell.

Are Lions Really Afraid of Kitchen Chairs?

The classic image of a lion tamer is a person holding a whip and a wooden kitchen chair while the lion cowers then swipes, unable to get to the trainer. But you only need to watch one animal documentary about the plains of Africa to realize that a chair is hardly going to be an obstacle for such a powerful cat. Is the formidable lion really afraid?

This style of lion taming was popularized by Clyde Beatty, a famous American animal trainer from the mid-1900s, although he claimed that it was in use when he started in the business.

Beatty believed that the lions weren't afraid of the chair; it just confused them. In thousands of years of evolutionary development, nothing like the shape of a chair would ever have been encountered by a lion, so they have no built-in mechanism or experience to deal with it. And like all cats, lions are single-minded, so the four legs of the chair waving in the lion's face are enough to make the lion lose focus and get confused. So, even if the lion were planning to kill the tamer, the chair would make it lose its train of thought and get distracted.

Adding to the mystique of the kitchen chair, lions are hierarchical, and the tamer spends a lot of time in the lion's cage, chair in hand, training the lion and demonstrating that the human is in charge.

Mind you, while the chair is effective in making the lion back down and be submissive, if the tamer makes a sudden move and pushes the chair too deep into the lion's personal space, then the lion will be inclined to defend itself and attack. It is then that a tamer will quickly realize that a flimsy four-legged wooden kitchen chair is no match at all for the king of the jungle.

Why Are the Upper Class Called Blue Bloods?

A blue blood is a member of a socially prominent and wealthy family, and the term is generally reserved for the upper class of society. The term has existed for centuries, but given that nobody's blood is actually blue, how did it originate?

Blue blood is the translation of the Spanish *sangre azul*, which relates to aristocrats who lived in Castile, Spain, centuries ago.

From their invasion in the 8th century, the Moors, who were from North Africa and had dark skin, ruled over much of Spain. Many interracial marriages took place, but many of the oldest families from Castile avoided intermarriage.

As a result, the Castilians thought of themselves as pure and remained extremely fair skinned, making their veins appear a profoundly blue color against their white skin. They called themselves the *sangre azul*—the blue bloods.

The term was later used in England to describe the nobility before it became globally recognized.

Can You Get Killed by Poking a Metal Object into a Power Outlet?

Many people, particularly parents, wonder what would happen if a child were to stick a metal object into a power outlet. It can't be that big a deal, can it? If it were, there'd be more compulsory protection on the outlets, or they'd be located out of a child's reach. Is it actually dangerous?

You bet.

If you poke a metal object into the larger slot on the left, or the small, round hole at the bottom, nothing should happen. These are the neutral and ground slots and should not be dangerous. The smaller slot on the right, however, is the hot slot from which the current flows, and if you poke a metal object in there, you will likely receive an electrical shock.

The human body is about 70 percent water, which makes it an excellent conductor of electricity. Electricity seeks a quick path to the earth, so if you are standing on the ground and are not wearing insulated footwear, you're in for a real shock. If you have wet skin and are standing in a puddle of water, the shock will be even more severe.

As a minimum, you may experience a headache, muscle spasms, unconsciousness, and breathing difficulties. Some of the more serious side effects include severe burns, brain damage, respiratory failure, cardiac arrest, and death.

According to the US Consumer Product Safety Commission, approximately four thousand people per year are taken to an emergency room seeking treatment for injuries caused by electrical outlets. Nearly 50 percent of these patients are children who have poked something into an outlet. And these are just the ones who are treated. Hundreds of people never even make it to the emergency room. Don't stick metal (or any) objects into power outlets.

Why Do Kamikaze Pilots Wear Helmets?

Kamikaze is the Japanese word meaning divine wind, named after a typhoon that is said to have saved Japan from a Mongol invasion in 1281. After the attacks of the Japanese air force on the Allies' ships in World War II, "kamikaze" has universally come to mean a suicide pilot.

Toward the end of the war, the Allies began advancing toward Japan, and Japanese aircraft were often outnumbered and outclassed, resulting in a scarcity of adept pilots. At the same time, the Japanese air force was assigned the task of assisting the Japanese ships in the Leyte Gulf. The task was larger than could be accommodated, so Vice Admiral Takijiro Onishi formed a Kamikaze Special Attack Force. There were many volunteers to be pilots, but many experienced and valuable pilots were turned away, with most kamikaze pilots being young university students. Ceremonies were often held before such missions, during which the pilots were given medals of honor. Approximately six thousand Japanese soldiers died in the kamikaze missions, and all are thought to have been volunteers.

Given that the kamikaze pilots knew they were going to die, people sometimes wonder why they wore helmets. In fact, the helmets weren't worn to protect the pilots from dying, but to protect them from injuries during the flight so that they could reach the target, to keep their heads warm, and because the helmets housed radio earphones. The helmets merely helped the pilots to complete their missions because the helmets were necessary to pilot the aircraft. In addition, many missions were unsuccessful; if failure was likely, pilots were encouraged to return to base and the helmets assisted with this. Some say that pilots didn't wear helmets at all at that time, but merely wore leather flight caps and goggles. If so, these were worn for the same reasons—to help the pilot complete the mission.

Is There Really a Calm before the Storm?

Sometimes at the end of a hot and humid afternoon, everything will suddenly go quiet. The air becomes still, and even the birds stop singing. This is the calm before the storm. A few minutes later the air changes again, the clouds darken and lower, and the storm hits. Why does this happen?

Most storms need warm, moist air for fuel. This air is drawn up to the clouds from the surrounding environment as the storm system develops, leaving a low-pressure vacuum close to the ground. The air travels up through and over the clouds before it descends back down to lower altitudes, pulled by the vacuum that remains. On the way back down, the air becomes warmer and drier. When that warm, stable air spreads across an area, it makes the rest of the air stable. That is the calm before the storm.

This process does not always happen, and there are many different types of storms. Some don't produce a calming influence at all, and instead are preceded by powerful winds and thunder.

Are Computer Games as Addictive as Cocaine?

"It could be a lot worse; they could be into drugs." Comments such as this are common when parents describe the habits of their teenage children, one of which is playing computer games. The problem is that many experts liken gaming to drug use.

Some Chinese experts refer to video games as "digital heroin," while others in the United States have called it "electronic cocaine." In 2016, the former executive director of the rehab clinic The Dunes East Hampton, Dr. Nicholas Kardaras, said, "I have found it easier to treat heroin and crystal meth addicts than lost-in-the-matrix video gamers or Facebook-dependent social media addicts."

But are computer games actually addictive, causing real changes in the brain the way drugs such as cocaine do? Yes, but only to a degree.

Dopamine is a neurotransmitter in the brain that increases when we experience something pleasurable. For our ancestors, it served as an important survival benefit, rewarding a successful or beneficial behavior that promoted well-being, such as finding a meal or a mate.

Scientists have found that when computer games are played, particularly ones with progressing levels of challenge, dopamine is released as a reward response to achievement. The dopamine signals to the brain that it has succeeded in the challenge, and this prompts the brain to want to repeat the action to receive more pleasure in the form of dopamine. As each new level of the game poses a greater challenge, even more dopamine will be released when it is successfully negotiated. A 1998 study by a team of scientists in London, England, led by Professor Matthias Koepp found that the dopamine levels in subjects playing video games increased 100 percent.

Drug use produces a similar response in the brain, and the euphoric effect from cocaine is the direct result of an increase in dopamine. Cocaine elevates dopamine in the brain to such a high level that, as the drug wears off and the dopamine is reduced, the person seeks to restore it by taking more cocaine. This can result in an addiction, the same way a computer game can become addictive.

But are the levels of dopamine production and addiction potential the same for computer games and cocaine? No. To put it into perspective, here is a list of activities and the amount dopamine increases for each:

Eating food—100 percent

Playing computer games—100 percent

Having sex—200 percent

Taking cocaine—350 percent

Taking methamphetamine—1,200 percent

To answer the question, yes, playing computer games increases dopamine levels and can be addictive, but to a far lesser extent than taking drugs. So, don't worry if your teenage children are playing the odd computer game—just make sure they're not eating and having sex at the same time, as that could definitely lead to a serious addiction.

Did Einstein Really Fail Math as a Child?

Albert Einstein was a German-born theoretical physicist who developed the groundbreaking theory of relativity, which explains how space, time, and gravity interact, and is widely thought to be one of the pillars of modern physics. He is widely regarded as the most famous scientist in history, but there are commonly held beliefs about his childhood that conflict with the genius that he was. One particular myth states that Einstein was not a good student and that he actually flunked math. Is there any truth to this outlandish claim? How could he have completed the work he did without being good at math?

In 1935, a rabbi at Princeton showed Einstein a clipping of a newspaper column with the headline "Greatest living mathematician failed in mathematics." Einstein just laughed at that suggestion and went on to explain that he never failed math, and that in primary school he was at the top of his class. By age eleven, he was reading college physics textbooks, and his sister said that by age twelve he was solving complicated problems in arithmetic as well as learning algebra and geometry by himself with textbooks his parents bought him. In addition to learning the content of these books themselves, he used them to solve new theories, coming up with a unique way of proving the Pythagorean theorem. Before he was fifteen, he had mastered differential and integral calculus. Clearly a gifted child, his favorite book at age thirteen was Kant's *Critique of Pure Reason*.

The answer to the question is that, no, Einstein did not fail math as a child, and was in fact exceptional at the subject. So, where did this idea come from?

It probably originated from the fact that at age sixteen he failed the entrance exam to the Zurich Polytechnic. However, he was nearly two years from graduating high school at the time and had not learned much and did not know much French, which was the language in which the exam was written.

Einstein did hate his early years at school, particularly the strict protocols and rote learning demanded of students. And he skipped classes and angered professors because he preferred to study on his own. Despite all of that, he was an exceptional math student and gained high marks from an early age.

If anyone did doubt his math ability, in 1921 he received the Nobel Prize in Physics "for his services to theoretical physics, and especially for his discovery of the law of the photoelectric effect," which was a pivotal step in the evolution of quantum theory. If any of that makes any sense to you, you will know that it requires some pretty advanced math equations.

Why Do People Rub Their Eyes When They're Tired?

We've all seen young children clench a fist, rub it vigorously into their eye, then start yawning. There's no surer sign that it's time for bed, but why the eye rubbing?

Here are a few physiological reasons for this behavior:

- As a person gets tired, the eyes get fatigued, as well. By rubbing the eyes, eyelids, and muscles around the eyes, the soreness and tension are relieved. It's similar to rubbing a sore arm muscle after playing sports.

- Tired eyes are dry eyes. Having been exposed to air for a long period of time, the lubricating film that bathes the front of the eyes in a protective layer begins to evaporate. Rubbing the eyes stimulates the lacrimal glands, which then produce more fluid to bring moisture to the eyes and provide some relief.
- There's a connection between the muscles that move the eyes and the heart. Applying pressure to the eyes stimulates the vagus nerve, which causes a reflex that actually slows down the heart rate and relaxes you. This can make you even more tired.

So, the next time your toddlers rub their eyes, it's time for bed, despite whatever protests or excuses might be made.

Does Speaking to Plants Encourage Them to Grow?

Many people maintain that talking to plants, and exposing them to melodious sounds generally, encourages them to grow and promotes health. Indeed, music has been recorded specifically for the purpose of invigorating plant growth.

A number of scientific studies have been conducted in an attempt to prove this. One study found that ultrasonic vibrations stimulated the production of hormones in plants and encouraged growth, while others have discovered that sounds that fall within the range of human hearing also led to increased growth.

There have also been studies carried out to determine which type of music produces the best results, suggesting that classical music made plants healthier, whereas loud rock music was detrimental to their health. One such study indicated that extremely loud noises increased the germination rate of some plants.

It was suggested as early as the 19th century that plants are capable of emotions and are likely to be healthier if they receive a lot of attention. It has also been claimed that, while they evidently can't understand the spoken word, plants are capable of understanding the meaning behind speech. Charles Darwin even compared certain characteristics of primates with those of plants.

Proponents of the theory that talking to plants encourages growth argue that such action involves respiration, providing the plants with extra carbon dioxide, which they need in order to grow. In addition, if a plant's owner speaks to it on a regular basis, he or she is likely to notice things wrong with it—such as pest infestation—and can then deal with them before they cause a serious problem.

Despite the many studies and theories on the topic, there is thought to be no scientific evidence to suggest that playing music or talking to plants will increase their growth rate or make them healthier.

Why Do Women Dance More than Men?

If you go to any place where there's a dance floor, you will notice a lot more women dancing than men. Women dance with men when they can but seem equally happy to dance alone or in groups of women. Men, on the other hand, are usually very reluctant to strut their stuff, and often only do so under duress. Is there a reason for this marked disparity between the sexes?

Women dance for pure pleasure. They often see dancing as a form of self-expression and not as a talent show, not caring about what other people think of their style. Men, on the hand, usually derive very little joy from the mere act of dancing and only want to dance if they can dance well. They often feel they are being judged on their style, so they think they should either dance like an expert, or not dance at all.

These different mindsets exist for a reason. As is often the case, evolution provides the most plausible explanation.

Scientists believe that early humans danced to bond and communicate as part of a courtship display. To dance well requires good health, coordination, rhythm, stamina, and strength. Skillful dancing may have indicated genetic fitness and the ability to produce and better provide for offspring. These qualities would have likely made someone more attractive to the opposite sex and given them an evolutionary advantage.

As with most species in the animal kingdom, our ancestral females, limited by the number of offspring they could have, sought quality over quantity. Dancing was one key way to determine the best mate. This may have led women to dance more, attempting to entice the men to dance so they could see what the men were made of. Dancing up close would have also

194

given the women an opportunity to garner further information from the men, including pheromones, to assess whether they were a good match.

Our ancestral males pursued the females, seeking quantity over quality so as to increase the chances of propagating his genes. The need to impress the female may have given him a fear of dancing, because he knew he had to dance well, or risk being shunned. There was a lot to lose, so only men who were very good dancers would have taken the risk. Women, on the other hand, were being pursued, so they had nothing to lose if they danced badly, and everything to gain by using it as a tool to obtain information about a potential suitor.

Because of this early social dynamic, most women evolved to love dancing, while most men evolved to hate it. And you only need to look at any dance floor in America to realize the truth behind this hypothesis; it was surely a man who wrote the Scissor Sisters song "I Don't Feel Like Dancing."

How Did the Term "Bootlegging" Originate?

"Bootlegging" refers to smuggling or otherwise acquiring goods without the payment of taxes or royalties. Black market CDs and DVDs are typical bootlegged items—they are sold without the permission of the copyright holder.

The term was frequently used in the United States during the Prohibition era of the 1920s and '30s. During this time, when the sale of alcohol was not allowed, there was an enormous black market for illegal alcohol. Bootleggers smuggled alcohol into the country and sold it without paying any taxes. Bootlegging is different from moonshining, which is the practice of illegally selling homemade alcohol, sometimes known as "white lightning."

The term "bootlegging" has been in existence since the late 1800s and derives from the trick of concealing something illegal, often a bottle of alcohol, down the leg of a high boot. This practice is thought to have originated with pirates, who wore knee-high boots, which they used to conceal some extra booty for themselves instead of sharing it with the rest of the crew.

❓ Why Does Time Fly When You're Having Fun?

It's such a common complaint—you sit at work completely bored all day, and the minutes seem like hours, yet when you go on vacation it seems to pass in the blink of an eye. "Time flies when you're having fun," people often say, but is there any science to this phenomenon?

Psychologists believe that people do perceive time differently depending on their mental state and what they are doing. When people are bored and uninterested, their minds tend to wander. When this happens, people usually look at the time very regularly to see how much longer it will be until they can do something they enjoy. Conversely, when people are busily engaged in an enjoyable activity, their minds are focused, and they don't look at the clock as often. The more often you check the time, the slower it seems to pass, and vice versa. These findings were recorded in a 2003 study by Dinah Avni-Babad and Ilana Ritov, "Routine and the Perception of Time," published in the *Journal of Experimental Psychology: General*.

Paradoxically, though time flies while you're having fun, your memory perception of that time is usually the opposite. When you think back on an interesting passage of time, it generally involves a lot of new experiences or memorable moments. You are able to retrieve many of those moments from your memory, so in retrospect, it feels as if the time lasted a lot longer. On the other hand, long, boring days when you did nothing, which felt like an eternity at the time, will feel like they flew by when you remember them, as they added very little new information to your memory. Perhaps the mark of a successful life, then, is that while the days flew by, the years felt long and interesting.

While time definitely does fly when you're having fun, there's another factor to consider, according to psychologists Alan Kingstone and Anthony Chaston from the University of Alberta. They conducted a study where participants were asked to look for a given object in a certain time frame. Because of the time pressure they were under, the subjects reported that time had seemed to pass very quickly. This same experience is often reported by students who are under time pressure during an exam, or people working at a hectic job where they struggle to complete their required tasks.

Given that stressful, time-pressured activities such as taking an exam are not usually considered "fun" by most people, perhaps the expression should really be "time flies when you're attentively engaged and focused in any activity, whether you derive pleasure from it or not." Not quite as catchy as the original, is it?

Do Cats Always Land on Their Feet?

On the rare occasion that you see a cat lose its balance and fall, it will invariably perform an acrobatic twist in the air before landing on its feet unscathed. How do they manage such an incredible feat, and do they always land on their feet?

The technique, known as the cat righting reflex, is the cat's innate ability to orient itself as it falls so that it lands on its feet. Most cats perfect the reflex by six weeks of age.

French scientist Étienne-Jules Marey first recorded the reflex in 1890, by dropping a cat and using a camera to capture its fall in a rapid series of images. He later watched in slow motion to determine how the cat managed to land on its feet.

Marey determined that a vestibular apparatus in the cat's inner ear acts as its orientation compass so that it knows which way is up. Once this is determined, it rotates its head to see where to land. Then the cat's unique skeletal structure comes into play. Cats don't have a collarbone, and they have an unusually flexible backbone with thirty vertebrae, as opposed to the twenty-four in humans. This gives the cat added mobility, allowing it to arch its back as it positions its front feet underneath its body, with the front paws close to the face to protect it from impact.

The minimum height for the righting reflex to be effective is about 12 inches. Any higher than that and they will almost always land on their feet. But height is a factor in whether a cat lands without injury. When a cat lands, its legs bear the bulk of the impact, but owing to their low volume-to-weight ratio which allows them to reduce their speed while falling, this impact is lessened. Strangely, a 1987 study of 132 cats published in the *Journal of the American Veterinary Medical Association* found that cats were actually less likely to suffer severe injuries when they fell from a height of more than seven stories than when they fell from between two and seven stories. It was thought that after falling five stories, the cat attains its top speed, after which it relaxes and spreads its body widely to increase air drag. However, critics of the study pointed out a sampling error in that fatal falls were not included, as an already-dead cat would not be taken to the vet. Most experts now agree with the conclusion of a 2003 study of 119 cats that was published in the *Journal of Feline Medicine and Surgery*. It concluded that falls from more than seven stories were more likely to result in severe injury or death. Even though the cat is able to right itself and land on its feet, its legs are not able to absorb all the shock from such a fall.

So, while a cat will always land on its feet, it won't always survive; luckily, they've got nine lives. Of course, if you really want to test a cat's righting reflex, strap a piece of buttered toast to its back.

Will You Get Tetanus by Standing on a Rusty Nail?

Remember when you were a kid and you stood on a rusty nail, or anything rusty, and your mother would go into a blind panic that you were about to contract tetanus? The next thing you knew, you were being raced off to the doctor to get a shot. Were these fears justified, or is the rusty nail-tetanus proposition yet another common fallacy?

Tetanus is an infection of the nervous system with the *Clostridium tetani* bacteria. Spores of this bacteria are found in soil and animal feces. The spores can remain infectious in the soil for forty years. Tetanus is contracted when the spores enter your body through a wound and become active bacteria. The bacteria spreads through the bloodstream and makes a poison called tetanus toxin, which blocks nerve signals from reaching your muscles, causing severe muscular spasms.

So, do rusty nails give you tetanus? Stepping on a rusty nail can give you tetanus, but so can stepping on a new nail. Either can potentially give you tetanus if they're dirty because it is the dirt, and not the rust, that may contain the dangerous spores. The reason behind the rusty-nail fear is that if a nail has been outside long enough to get rusty, then it's more likely to have been exposed to soils containing the bacteria, and the crevices on the rust provide a place for the soil to lodge and remain. *Clostridium tetani* can only reproduce in an oxygen-deprived setting like a puncture wound, which standing on a rusty nail would provide.

Most cases of tetanus in the United States occur in people who have not been vaccinated against it, and in these cases, without treatment, one out of three people will die.

Why Do Superheroes Wear Their Underwear on the Outside?

Over the years, many male superheroes have been known for one particular costume characteristic—wearing a pair of color-contrasting underwear on top of their pants. It became normal to see Superman's red underwear over his blue pants, or Batman's black underwear over his gray uniform. Is this bizarre phenomenon merely a fashion faux pas that persisted? Did they lack fashion role models because they lost their parents at an early age, or was it to distract people from focusing on how much they actually looked like their daytime persona? Just how did this superhero clothing convention begin?

It wasn't a mistake. Early superheroes were modeled on the circus performers and wrestlers of the time, who often wore trunks over a set of tights. Since superheroes are generally associated with feats of athleticism and strength, it was logical to emulate the garb of these real-life athletes. Two of the earliest examples of this were Flash Gordon in 1934 and Superman in 1938. Julius Schwartz, the editor of *DC Comics* (which included Superman) from 1944 to 1986, confirmed this as the origin of the practice.

But at the risk of pedantry, it should be noted that the outer layer of clothing was not actually underwear. It was tight underwear-like shorts worn over even tighter leggings. And that makes it all OK.

🔮 Why Do Pirates Love Parrots?

The depiction of pirates with parrots perched on their shoulders stems from the character of Long John Silver in Robert Louis Stevenson's 1883 novel, *Treasure Island*. Stevenson admitted that he got the idea from Daniel Defoe's groundbreaking 1719 work, *Robinson Crusoe*, in which the stranded narrator captures a parrot and keeps it as a pet, but *Treasure Island* popularized the concept. Ever since that time, the pop culture conception of pirates has involved parrots. But that's fiction. Was it ever the case in fact?

Yes, according to Colin Woodard, author of the 2008 book *The Republic of Pirates: Being the True and Surprising Story of the Caribbean Pirates and the Man Who Brought Them Down.* "The parrot trope is almost certainly grounded in reality," Woodard claims. But how? And why?

During the Golden Age of Piracy in the 17th and 18th centuries, pirates sailed throughout the Atlantic Ocean, pillaging anyone they came across. They generally followed the trade routes, often making stops in the Caribbean and Central America, where parrot populations were large. The exotic pet trade in Europe, especially in London and Paris, was booming at the time, with rich people paying a lot of money for unusual animals. The pirates knew this, and when they saw these colorful birds, the only color they really saw was gold. They bought or stole the birds from market vendors and transported them back to the European world for sale. Parrots and parrot cages have been found listed among the inventory of ships from that time.

While the birds were shipped more often than they were kept as personal pets, they did provide the added bonus of enjoyable companionship while aboard. The pirates undertook long and boring voyages, and exotic pets provided an interesting distraction. Monkeys were fairly common on ships, as well. Parrots had the advantage of being intelligent, eating seeds that could be easily stored, having bright and colorful plumage, and mimicking sounds to entertain the pirates and impress onlookers when in port. Because of these factors, it is likely that a number of parrots were actually kept by the pirates rather than sold.

❓ Do Cell Phones Really Interfere with Aircraft?

"Please set all portable electronic devices, including any cell phones, to flight mode." How many times have you heard this? At the start and end of every flight. Most people comply with the instruction without being completely sure why. The general assumption is that the signals from cell phones interfere with the plane's navigational instruments, which might cause the plane to crash. Yet many people forget to turn their phones off, and the plane doesn't crash. This raises the question—can a cell phone really bring down a plane?

The Federal Communications Commission has banned the use of cell phones on aircraft, but that ban is to prevent the disruption to cellular towers on the ground. When a call is made from the air, the signal bounces off multiple available cell towers, rather than one at a time. This may result in the ground networks becoming clogged up. So, no danger to the plane there.

However, the Federal Aviation Association has banned the use of cell phones because of potential electromagnetic interference with the aircraft systems, caused by the signals cell phones emit. These may interrupt the normal operation of the plane's instruments, in particular the communication and navigation systems, and potentially the flight controls (such as autopilot) and warning systems.

But has this ever happened?

According to the International Air Transport Association, seventy-five instances of suspected electronic device interference occurred between 2003 and 2009. While these instances could not be definitively validated, the pilots who reported the incidents claimed that once the passengers were then instructed to turn off their electronic devices, the issues were resolved. That said, there is no known example of an air accident having been caused by the use of a cell phone. But it's also impossible to say that some accidents may not have been caused this way.

In a 2013 article in *CNN Travel* titled "Can Your Cell Phone Bring Down a Plane?", Kenny Kirchoff, an engineer at Boeing's Electromagnetic Interference Lab in Seattle, said that the issue is not necessarily that a phone can bring down a plane, but that a phone can interfere with the plane and cause more work for the pilots during the critical phases of flight. This may cause a pilot to get distracted, lowering the overall level of safety on the plane.

On balance, it's likely that cell phones can interfere with an aircraft, but only to a small degree. And if the risks were significant and life-threatening, the policy would be far more strictly enforced, or phones would be banned from aircraft entirely. That said, the consequences could be dire, so for the skeptics out there, perhaps this is one of those cases where it's better to be safe than sorry.

Why Do You Never See Baby Pigeons?

In cities all around the world, thousands of pigeons are seen in large flocks on the streets and in the squares, but all of them are adult. So, where are all the baby pigeons? Many other infant animals are commonly seen, but never baby pigeons.

Of course, baby pigeons do exist; it's just that they're hidden in their nests, which pigeons build in high-up places, on ledges and on the tops of buildings. Both the male and female incubate their eggs, which hatch after just eighteen days. Baby pigeons need a lot of care from their parents and are fed by both their mother and their father. The parents don't need to leave the nest; they feed their young with a glandular secretion called "pigeon milk," a high-protein food that promotes rapid growth in the baby birds.

During this nesting time, adult pigeons are very territorial and ward off any strangers from their nests, while the baby pigeons remain in the nest and are cared for by their parents until they can fend for themselves. Once this happens, they leave the nest and roam the streets with the other birds. At this stage, they are a similar size to adult pigeons, although they don't reach sexual maturity until five or six months of age. So, the truth is that young pigeons are in plain view, although by the time they leave the nest, it's difficult to distinguish them from the adult pigeons.

Why Are Rabbits Associated with Easter?

Every Easter, millions of children (and a lot of chocolate-loving adults) bite the heads off their Easter Bunnies with glee. But why did this animal become associated with Easter in the first place?

The exact reason the rabbit was selected is uncertain. In general, the animal is known to be a prolific procreator and was an ancient symbol of fertility and new life.

People of ancient times believed that the hare and rabbit were hermaphrodites and could reproduce without copulating, probably because these animals can conceive a second litter of offspring while still pregnant with the first. This led to an association with the Virgin Mary and inclusion of the hare in religious symbolism.

Some suggest that the Easter Bunny derives from Ostara, the ancient Germanic fertility goddess. Ostara was the friend of all children and had a pet rabbit that laid brightly colored eggs that Ostara gave as gifts. Ostara then became associated with Easter owing to the theory that the word Easter came from Eostre, a version of the name Ostara.

Originally called the Easter Hare, the concept likely originated with the German Lutherans, with whom the animal played the role of judge, determining whether children had been good or bad at the start of the season of Eastertide. The legend has it that the Hare would then carry colored eggs in a basket and deliver them to children who had been good,

similar to Santa Claus at Christmas. The earliest reference to an Easter Bunny carrying eggs was in a 1572 German text that read "Do not worry if the Easter Bunny escapes you; should we miss his eggs, we will cook the nest." The custom was then mentioned in a 1682 text by the German physician Georg Franck von Franckenau.

Candy shaped as rabbits became a fixture in American stores starting in the 19th century, a century after German immigrants introduced the Easter Bunny to the US. This practice soon spread worldwide before the rabbits turned into chocolate.

 ## Are Women Better Multitaskers than Men?

Multitasking is the ability to perform more than one task simultaneously or over a short period. Much to the chagrin of men, the idea that women are better multitaskers has been a long-held societal belief.

While people may become better at multitasking through practice, most experts who believe that women have an enhanced ability put it down to the evolutionary hunter-gatherer hypothesis. This theory says that while our male ancestors typically focused on one linear task at a time, such as hunting, women had to juggle a number of tasks, like gathering food, preparing meals, and tending to infant children. These skills were passed down over thousands of years, so the brains of today's women are wired to be better at multitasking.

Critics of this theory, who are mostly men, say that the evidence to support it is purely anecdotal, and a number of the studies carried out on the topic are inconclusive or do not reflect real-life conditions. Indeed, one Swedish study found that men actually outperformed women in this area.

But in 2013, a group of psychologists from the University of Hertfordshire, the University of Glasgow, and the University of Leeds, all in Britain, conducted two detailed experiments, determined to find out the truth. Led by Dr. Gijsbert Stoet, in the first experiment they compared 120 men and 120 women in a computer test that involved switching between tasks involving shape-recognition and counting. The sexes performed equally when the tasks were done one at a time, but when the tasks were mixed up, a clear difference appeared. All the subjects slowed down and made more mistakes, but the men were significantly slower, taking 77 percent longer to respond, compared to the women, who took 69 percent longer.

The second test was more practical. The subjects were given eight minutes to complete a series of tasks, including answering a ringing phone, doing simple math problems, locating restaurants on a map, and deciding how to search for a lost key in a field. It was impossible to complete all the tasks in the allotted time, so it forced the subjects to prioritize and remain calm under stress. On the whole, the women outperformed the men, and in the lost key task in particular, they scored much higher. While the men were seen to act impulsively, the women were observed to possess a higher level of cognitive control than the men, planning and organizing better when under pressure.

In the end, the researchers concluded that while some men are experts in the field, the average woman is better able to organize her time and switch quickly between tasks than the average man—that is, she is better at multitasking.

❓ Why Don't Women Faint as Much as They Used To?

If you watch any period drama from the 1800s, the women seem to drop like flies, struggling to maintain consciousness when confronted with the slightest emotional shock. These days, women rarely faint at all. Have women evolved to lose the fainting gene, or is something else really going on?

Here are a number of explanations for this era's fainting disparity:

Corsets. Women in Victorian times often wore corsets, made of tightly woven fabric with vertical rib inserts and fastened at the back with tight laces. These garments were worn to give a flat look to the stomach and to accentuate certain bodily curves. But they also made it hard for the wearer to breathe or eat (because it was hard to get food down, or the stomach was so compressed that it couldn't hold much food), and the woman's heart was unable to pump as freely. During times of heightened emotional arousal, the body needs more oxygen to fuel the fight-or-flight reflex, and the corset prevented this. A woman wearing a corset in such circumstances wouldn't have been able to breathe as well, and with potentially low blood sugar from a lack of food, she would have been more likely to get lightheaded and faint.

Heat and weight. Women of that era also wore an enormous amount of clothing, even in summer. In addition to the corset, they wore underwear, a full skirt, a petticoat, and a bonnet. Bearing the excess weight, women may have overheated more than today, causing them to faint more readily.

Poisoning. During the 19th century, arsenic was widely used in the manufacture of everything from fabrics to paints to wallpaper to makeup. Lead was also a common ingredient in makeup and hair dyes. These prevalent toxins could have resulted in the chronic poisoning of women, who swooned and fainted as a consequence.

Femininity. While all of the above factors may well have contributed to a higher incidence of fainting in yesteryear, it is highly likely that many fainting fits were simply put on. Women, particularly those of high standing, were expected to play the role of the delicate flower, and it was considered ladylike to faint if their slightest sensibility was offended. These days, fainting is generally seen as a sign of weakness. That fact alone may have been enough to quash the pastime.

Can Piranhas Really Devour a Cow in under a Minute?

Piranhas are among the most feared aquatic animals on earth. One of the reasons for this is President Theodore Roosevelt. When visiting Brazil in 1913, Teddy witnessed the piranha at work and reported what he saw in his 1914 book, *Through the Brazilian Wilderness*. He described the fish as the "embodiment of evil ferocity." What he had seen was a school of piranhas in the Amazon River tearing a cow apart and eating it to the bone in a matter of minutes. What he didn't realize was that the local fishermen had created the spectacle by blocking off part of the river and starving the fish for several days before pushing a dead cow into the water. But Roosevelt was a famous man, and his story was widely read. The legend of the piranha had begun, and in the ensuing years, Hollywood did the rest. So, can they do it?

The most vicious of the twenty species found in the Amazon is the red-bellied piranha. It is around 10 inches long and weighs about 3 pounds. But it's got some teeth. Its teeth are only about a quarter inch long, but they're like razors, spaced in an interlocking pattern that cut like scissors. They also have incredibly strong jaws, capable of severing a human toe in one bite, and their muscular bodies allow for extremely rapid bursts of speed. In addition, piranhas don't chew. They bite off a chunk of flesh, which they immediately swallow, allowing them to bite off another chunk without delay.

These anatomical factors make the piranha an impressive predator, but their real strength is in numbers. They eat in schools of hundreds, continuously rotating during the feeding frenzy. They take turns at biting with incredible speed, often giving the water a boiling effect. But they only eat like this when they're starving, like in the scene that Roosevelt witnessed. So, while they are able to strip a beast quickly to its skeleton, they will only do so in very specific circumstances.

In reality, piranhas pose very little threat to humans or any large animals. They are extremely timid omnivores, usually scavenging on plants or dead or dying animals, and the main reason they travel in large schools is for protection via safety in numbers. They are certainly not in the habit of attacking living things that are many times their own size.

But if those very specific circumstances do exist, featuring a starving shoal of hundreds of piranhas, you'd best not get in the water. It has been estimated that a human could be stripped of flesh in five minutes by between three and five hundred fish.

A cow would take a little longer, but they could do it. And whether it takes one minute or ten minutes really seems beside the point.

What Are the Origins of the Mexican Wave?

Known in the United States as simply "the wave," the Mexican wave takes place in sporting stadiums around the world when a large crowd acts in unison, with the people standing up in turn and throwing their arms in the air to create the effect of a wave traveling across the group. Just how did this strange pastime begin?

The wave was the brainchild of professional cheerleader "Krazy" George Henderson. At a major league baseball game between the Oakland Athletics and the New York Yankees on October 15, 1981, Krazy George explained to three sections of the crowd what he wanted to happen. The first couple of wave attempts broke down, but after much booing by the rest of the crowd, by the fourth attempt, a continuous wave swept around the entire stadium.

There is, however, a rival claimant. Former *Entertainment Tonight* host Robb Weller says that he and Dave Hunter led the first wave at a football game at the University of Washington's Husky Stadium in Seattle on October 31, 1981. Weller was an alumni cheerleader and Hunter was one of the band's trumpet players. The problem with this claim is that it occurred two weeks after Krazy George's debut, which was recorded for posterity on national television, the announcers even commenting on it. It is generally believed that Weller simply borrowed the idea after seeing Krazy George do it.

That said, the University of Washington certainly helped to popularize the wave, as it was used for all the Huskies' home games in 1981. From there, it spread to other universities, and then to the Detroit Tigers' baseball games in 1984, a season in which they won the World Series, gaining the wave even more national attention. The wave then got a large amount of publicity at the 1984 Los Angeles Olympics, but it wasn't until the 1986 FIFA World Cup in Mexico that the wave received international acclaim. That event earned the wave its longer name.

A 2002 study conducted by Tamás Vicsek at the Eötvös Loránd University in Hungary found that a wave has to be initiated, never occurs spontaneously, and requires a minimum of twenty-five people acting in concert to get going. It also found that waves in the Northern Hemisphere almost always go clockwise. No comment was made about the direction of Southern Hemisphere waves.

But whatever your view of the wave, halt one at your peril. If you're at a stadium and you and the people nearby refuse to join in, thereby breaking the wave, you will be met with a barrage of booing and jeering. Wave on.

Why Are Men in Charge of the Barbecue When Women Do Most of the Cooking?

In households throughout the Western world, the woman is in charge of the kitchen and all the cooking—except when it comes to the barbecue, that is. That's the man's domain. "Women cook, men grill." But what is it that makes grilling "men's work"?

In our early history, women foraged for certain foods, such as fruits, while men went out and hunted dangerous prey that was more difficult to come by. While the women did most of the cooking, the men tended to cook meat on ceremonial occasions following a big hunt. This has filtered through to modern times, where barbecuing is often seen as a special occasion.

Added to this is the thrill of grilling. It involves fire and sharp tools, lending an element of danger to which the testosterone-filled man is often drawn. The kitchen is boring, but the barbecue is exciting.

There's also the prehistoric bonding element of gathering around a fire. Grilling provides a good opportunity to hang out with other men and drink beer. The barbecue is seen as the guys' turf—it's their territory, and it acts as a sanctuary where they're able to talk freely among themselves.

Fire, meat, beers, men—these factors all create a strong connection between grilling and a sense of masculinity, as in the barbecue is dangerous, it is the man's domain, and only he shall cook on it.

But the main reason why men only cook on the barbecue and not in the kitchen? The barbecue requires very little in the way of cleaning up.

Do Alaska Natives Really Have Hundreds of Words for Snow?

The claim that the Alaska Natives have hundreds of words for snow is widespread but controversial. The idea came about as a result of anthropologist Franz Boas's travels through northern Canada in the 1880s to learn about the Alaska Natives. In his 1911 work, *Handbook of American Indian Languages*, Boas discussed the many words that the Alaska Natives used for snow, and the concept spread into popular culture. But is there actually any basis to the claim?

The two main Alaska Native languages, Inuit and Yupik, both have multiple dialects. This fact alone gives rise to many different words for snow. But these languages are able to spawn so many words for snow primarily because they're polysynthetic. Polysynthetic languages combine a limited set of roots with multiple word endings to create many stand-alone words. Where in English, a concept such as "snow falling heavily and settling on the ground" is expressed as a sentence, the Natives will use a single word. For example, the root word *tla* means "snow that falls." Adding suffixes to this root gives any number of new single words: *tlamo* (snow that falls in large wet flakes); *tlatim* (snow that falls in small flakes); *tlaslo* (snow that falls slowly); *tlapinti* (snow that falls quickly); *tlapa* (snow that falls as powder snow); and *tlayinq* (snow that falls and is mixed with mud). That's just to name a few.

This means that Alaska Natives don't just have hundreds of words for snow, they have hundreds of words for everything, as an almost limitless number of single words can be formed using this grammatical structure.

So, how many words for snow are there?

Some linguists claim that the Yupik language has at least forty distinct words for snow, while the Inuit language has fifty-three. But it depends on what constitutes different words. If you're talking about the root words for snow, it's a similar number to what we have in English, where there is snow, sleet, powder, blizzard, slush, and so on. In an analysis of the Alaska Native languages in 1991 by Professor Anthony Woodbury of the University of Texas in Austin, there were fifteen distinct root words for snow that would be considered separate words in English.

But if you're talking about the polysynthetic words, the number is limited only by an Alaska Native's imagination. And with little else to look at in those parts aside from snow, that could run pretty wild. Let's just hope they've come up with a combined word for "yellow snow not to be eaten under any circumstances."

Just How Safe Is Fort Knox?

Fort Knox is a US Army post south of Louisville in Kentucky. Used in various capacities as a military facility, it is best known as the site of the United States Bullion Depository. It houses a large portion of the country's gold reserves, estimated as 2.3

percent of all the gold ever refined throughout human history—over 4,500 metric tons, valued at more than $180 billion. Frequently referenced in popular culture, from criminal plots in James Bond to comedy routines by Abbott and Costello, this depository has also housed other valuables over the years, including the original Declaration of Independence, as well as large supplies of morphine and opium during World War II. It has become a symbol of the ultimate impregnable vault and has given rise to the phrase "as safe as Fort Knox." But is that expression correct? Just how safe is Fort Knox?

The depository, often itself known as Fort Knox, is a fortified vault. In 1933, President Franklin D. Roosevelt issued an order outlawing the private ownership of gold coins. This led to a vast increase in the gold held by the Federal Reserve, which needed a place to store it. As a result, the facility was constructed in 1936, with the gold vault alone costing $560,000 to build (around $12 million in today's terms).

The gold vault is lined with granite walls and protected by a 21-inch-thick blast-proof door that weighs 20 tons. This door, as well as another 21-inch-thick inner emergency door, is made of torch- and drill-resistant material. The vault casing is 25 inches thick. In order to the enter the vault, staff members are required to use separate permutations that only they know.

The facility itself is ringed with electric fences and guarded by the heavily armed United States Mint Police, as well as thirty thousand Fort Knox army personnel and their associated artillery, tanks, and attack helicopters. No visitors are allowed inside the depository grounds, which are further protected by alarms, video cameras, microphones, barbed razor wire, and mine fields.

So, just how safe is Fort Knox? Pretty safe.

❓ Is Laughter Really the Best Medicine?

Everyone enjoys a good laugh from time to time, but is it really the best medicine as many people claim? Can it actually improve your health?

It seems so. The benefits of laughter are many and varied.

- **Relaxing the body.** Laughing relieves physical tension in the muscles, stimulates circulation, and thereby reduces stress.
- **Boosting the immune system.** Laughter does this by decreasing stress hormones and increasing the release of neuropeptides, a chemical that helps fight stress and improve your resistance to disease.
- **Triggering the release of endorphins.** This provides a feeling of well-being and has the ability to relieve pain.
- **Protecting the heart.** By increasing blood flow, laughter improves the function of blood vessels and helps protect against cardiovascular problems.
- **Burning calories.** This improves overall well-being.
- **Strengthening relationships.** This can have a profound effect on mental and emotional health.

All of this is easy to say, but has any of it been proven?

In a 2014 study conducted at California's Loma Linda University, researchers assessed the short-term memory and stress levels of twenty adults in their sixties and seventies. One group sat silently while the other watched funny videos. The participants then took a memory test. Those who'd watched the funny videos performed significantly better, at 43.6 percent correct compared with 20.3 percent in the non-humor group. Saliva samples also showed that the humor group had considerably lower levels of the stress hormone cortisol.

Another study, from the University of Oxford in 2011, tested the impact that laughter had on the pain threshold of volunteers. One group was shown comedy videos while the other was shown boring videos. The comedy video subjects were then able to withstand up to 10 percent more pain than they had been able to before watching the videos. The boring video subjects were able to bear less pain than before. Professor Robin Dunbar, who led the research, said the type of laughter is important. In order to release the pain-relieving endorphins, a strong belly laugh is required; simply tittering or giggling has little effect.

In addition to benefiting the body physically, laughter also makes you feel good and improves your mood, increasing positivity and optimism, as well as reducing depression and anxiety. In fact, some experts believe that the physical act of laughing is what is needed, and that simulated laughter can be just as beneficial as the real thing.

So, whether you're faking it or not, it's no joke; laughter really might be the best medicine.

Why Do We Cry at Happy Endings?

How many times have you seen it—after a tumultuous emotional relationship where the outcome seems uncertain, the perfect couple is united at the end of the movie and is set to live happily ever after together? Cue the waterworks. Given that the ending is positive, what makes us respond with tears of joy?

- **Mixed emotions.** Happy tears may be coupled with some sadness. A parent at their child's graduation, for example, is filled with pride and happiness but also feels a sense of loss as the child moves away from home.

- **Safety.** Psychoanalyst Joseph Weiss proposed this view in his 1952 article "Crying at the Happy Ending." Often, we cry in films that depict loss, grief, or danger. But instead of crying while these events are occurring, we only cry when they are resolved in a satisfactory way. We may feel too imperiled to express our feelings while the situation is actually happening because our subconscious mind is engaged in surviving or mastering that danger. The emotions we feel about the situation are suppressed until we feel it's safe enough to express the feelings that we held at bay. Though it's just the characters in a movie going through the issues, we vicariously identify with the pain and express it as tears when it is resolved on the screen.

- **Equilibrium.** In 2014, psychologists at Yale University proposed that people respond to a happy experience with a negative reaction in order to restore their emotional equilibrium. After running a group of volunteers through various scenarios and measuring their responses to happy reunions or cute babies, the researchers found that those who expressed negative emotions, such as crying, to positive news, were able to moderate intense emotions more quickly and recover faster. This would have been helpful in the survival of our ancestors by allowing them to deal with an issue and, rather than dwell on it, move on quickly to overcome new adversities.

Whichever of these theories is correct, and it's likely a combination, the next time you cry at a happy ending, the underlying cause of the tears will not be about the ending itself but the triumph over conflict.

Why Were Duels Always Fought at Dawn?

It's so common in Western movies that it's almost become a cliché. One guy insults another guy, and the next thing you know, they're facing off with pistols at dawn. But why wait until the next morning? Why not just get on with it?

While duels were fought at other times of the day, dawn was the preferred time for a number of reasons:

- With the sun low in the sky, neither person's vision was hampered by the glaring light. During the day, the sun would be more likely to be behind one of them, making it far more difficult for the opponent.
- Dueling at dawn ensured privacy and made it less likely that any law enforcement officers would be awake to prevent the duel or arrest the participants.
- Dueling at night was impractical because it would generally be too hard for those dueling to see each other. Added to that, a lot of potential participants would have been drunk at night when the argument giving rise to the duel took place. Waiting until dawn forced an interval, allowing time to reconsider or sober up and call it off.

Dueling became such a serious pastime during the 18th century that in 1777, a group of Irish gentlemen drew up a set of dueling rules in a document called the *Code Duello*. This code was adopted throughout Ireland before spreading to England, Europe, and America, with only slight variations. The code contained twenty-six specific rules that leaned toward dueling at dawn. Rule 15 stated: "Challenges are never to be delivered at night, unless the party to be challenged intends leaving the place of offense before morning; for it is desirable to avoid all hot-headed proceedings." Rule 17 stated: "The challenged chooses his ground; the challenger chooses his distance; the seconds fix the time and terms of firing."

In 1838, former governor of South Carolina John Lyde Wilson published an American version of the code, called *The Code of Honor; or Rules for the Government of Principals and Seconds in Dueling*. While this code merely specified that "the time must be as soon as practicable," the tradition of dueling at dawn persisted.

If a Tree Falls in a Forest, Does It Make a Sound?

This is a famous philosophical experiment related to observation and reality: If a tree falls in a forest and no one is around to hear it, does it make a sound?

This conundrum has been posed for hundreds of years. In *A Treatise Concerning the Principles of Human Knowledge*, published in 1710, Irish philosopher George Berkeley first discussed the concept that trees in a garden only exist while there is somebody present to perceive them. Then, in 1883, an article in *The Chautauquan* asked: "If a tree were to fall on an island where there were no human beings, would there be any sounds?" The article went on to answer the question with: "No. Sound is the sensation excited in the ear when the air or other medium is set in motion." The current phrasing of the question originated in the 1910 book *Physics*, written by Charles Riborg Mann and George Ransom Twiss.

To answer the question, here are the philosophical and the physiological perspectives.

Metaphysics—The Philosophical View

As with many issues in philosophy, a number of questions are posed.

Can something exist outside of human perception? This argument proposes that if nobody is around to see, hear, touch, or smell a tree, it cannot be said to exist, because what is to say it exists when such an existence is unknown?

Can we assume that the unobserved world functions in the same way as the observed world? While many scientists claim that the presence of an observer has no impact on the sound that a falling tree may or may not make, this claim is impossible to prove.

What is the difference between what something is and how it appears? If a tree exists outside our perception, then it will produce sound waves when it falls. While these sound waves will occur on a mechanical level, sound as it is perceived by human sensation will not.

Physics—The Physiological View

From a scientific viewpoint, the tree and the sound exist regardless of whether they are being observed. This is regardless of whether anybody hears it. Sound is produced by pressure waves and the laws of physics apply whether we perceive the sound or not. The sound that a tree makes is defined by these laws, and the auditory sensation as it is perceived is secondary.

In physics, sound is not dependent upon perception, so a tree will make a sound when it falls, whether or not someone sees it.

So, what's the answer? It depends on how the concept of sound is interpreted. If we look at sound physically, the tree does make a sound in all situations, but if we look at sound as our ability to perceive it, then the tree only makes a sound if somebody is there to hear it. Either way, the question is impossible to either prove or disprove, which is what has made it such an enduring riddle.

Is There a Fine Line between Pleasure and Pain?

The Divinyls sang about it, but it's not just pop bands who've made the link. Philosophers from Aristotle to Descartes to Jeremy Bentham have been hypothesizing about the connection between pleasure and pain for centuries. Is there any basis for this, or is it just a catchy thing to say?

There is strong evidence of the biological connection between the neurochemical pathways used for the perception of both pleasure and pain. Both feelings originate from neurons in the same locations of the brain: the amygdala, the pallidum, and the nucleus accumbens. A functional relationship between pleasure and pain also exists, in that pain itself elicits analgesia, which is the relief from pain, effectively a form of pleasure. In a 1999 study conducted at the University of California, San Francisco, researchers found that in response to pain, the reward pathways of the brain activate pain relief by releasing opioids and dopamine. It had been previously thought that the release of dopamine was only associated with positive experiences, but the study, done on rats, showed that pain and its relief (pleasure) are actually linked. This can potentially explain why a painful stimulus that activates the release of opioids and dopamine may actually be experienced as rewarding.

Scientists have hypothesized that the relationship between the two perceptions likely provided an evolutionary advantage. The brain is limited and, for efficiency, tends to focus on its most frequently used pathways. Having a common pathway for both pleasure and pain could have simplified the way in which our ancestors interacted with the environment in order to best survive. The link may have made it easier to weigh a variety of decisions. For example, a person may have been willing to endure a small amount of pain in order to obtain a large reward of pleasure-inducing food. When a decision such as that is governed by the one pathway, a more coherent and beneficial answer would have been likely, leading to a greater chance of survival.

Why Do Gas Tank Gauges Take Longer to Go from Full to Half–Full than Half–Full to Empty?

It's a common complaint of motorists—you drive for hours and hours before the gas tank gauge gets to half-full, then before you know it, it's about to hit empty. Is this a trick of the mind, or does it actually happen that way?

It does happen that way, and here are the reasons why.

1. The shape of the tank. In many cars, gas gauges are controlled by a floating ball with a weight that is attached to a metal arm. When the ball is floating at the top, the gauge shows "full," and when it's at the bottom, the gauge shows "empty." However, this mechanism measures the depth of the fuel in the tank, not the amount. Many gas tanks are not a uniform shape, and if the tank is wide at the top and narrow at the bottom, in a V-shape, the gauge will drop slowly at first and more quickly as the gas gets lower.

2. Filling excesses. It is possible to fill the tank beyond the full level on the gauge. When the pump clicks off, you can always get another gallon or two in there, which many people do. This gives you a couple of bonus gallons that the gauge doesn't know are there, meaning that the first bit of gas used doesn't make the gauge move. Then, at the other end, there are a couple of gallons left at the bottom of the tank when the gauge hits empty. Tanks are designed this way in an attempt to stop people from overfilling (which can cause problems) or running out of gas.

These two factors make the gauge reduction speed vary more considerably from full to half-full than from half-full to empty. To put it into numbers, if a tank holds 30 gallons, the gauge will show full at 28 gallons and empty at 2 gallons, with half-full being 14 gallons. This means that 16 gallons have to be used before the gauge gets to half-full, then after only another 12 gallons it will read empty. In addition, many people don't run their tank down to empty, which means draining the second half will seem even quicker.

3. A manufacturer's trick. Some believe that car manufacturers make the gauges this way on purpose so that people, especially when test driving a car, don't see the needle suddenly drop. This may create a perception of low gas mileage and deter a potential buyer.

4. It's psychological. We've all heard the expression "a watched pot never boils." Well, the opposite is true of a gas gauge.

A driver who is conscious that the car's gas is getting low will have a tendency to constantly watch the gas gauge. This can make it appear to be going down much faster than when the tank was full and there was nothing to worry about.

Do Glasses Weaken Your Eyes?

The vast majority of people need glasses at some point in their lives to correct their vision, whether it's due to farsightedness (hyperopia), shortsightedness (myopia), or any other eye condition. Glasses are designed to correct the specific condition, yet there is a commonly held belief that wearing glasses too often will weaken your eyes and actually make things worse. Is there any basis to this?

Put simply, no. Glasses don't change the process of any eye condition.

The erroneous belief is based on the idea that wearing glasses makes your eyes lazy. Your eyes grow accustomed to wearing glasses, so that once you remove them, you can't see as well as before.

Glasses work to correct your vision, which means your eye muscles can relax. But when the glasses are removed, the muscles that bend and straighten the lens of your eye must suddenly

work harder than normal to make your eyes focus. This can make your vision blurry and make you feel disorientated or dizzy. However, your eyes will get used to working harder again and will adjust back. They won't be worse than before as a result of wearing the glasses.

Another reason people think that glasses increase eye deterioration is because when you're wearing them you can see clearly, so when you take them off, the contrasting blurriness is far more noticeable. In addition, most people's eyes are more flexible first thing in the morning, before they put their glasses on, and they are better at focusing than they are later in the day, when they take their glasses off. This leads some to believe that the glasses are responsible for making their vision worse.

The most probable reason behind the myth, however, is that vision generally deteriorates with age, regardless of whether you wear glasses or not. People who wear glasses for years discover that their eyes are not as good over time, but this is likely caused by the aging process rather than the glasses themselves. When wearers find that they need their glasses more often, it doesn't then follow that the glasses have worsened their vision.

Strangely, however, virtually no studies on the topic have been conducted.

So, while there may be many reasons to choose not to wear glasses, the fear that you're damaging your eyesight shouldn't be one of them. On the other side of the coin, glasses won't cure your poor vision either.

Does 80 Percent of a Person's Heat Really Escape from Their Head?

When it comes to bundling up on a cold winter's day, a warm hat is obligatory. After all, everybody knows that we lose 80 percent of our body heat through our head, or so they say. Is there any truth to this?

No. The head makes up about 10 percent of the body's surface area. To lose 80 percent of the body's heat, the head would have to lose more than forty times as much heat per square inch as every other part of the body. Richard Ingebretsen of the University of Utah School of Medicine believes that the real reason we lose heat through our head is that most of the time when we're outside in the cold, we're clothed…If you don't have a hat on, you lose heat through your head, just as you would lose heat through your legs if you were wearing shorts.

A number of studies have been conducted on the subject. In a study reported in the 2008 *BMJ* (formerly the *British Medical Journal*), participants were tested in cold water, sometimes with wet suits and sometimes with the head submerged. The study found that the heat loss from the head was proportional to the amount of exposed skin. A similar study in 2013 by Thea Pretorius from the University of Manitoba found similar results—having a person's head immersed in cold water only added 10 percent to the person's overall heat loss.

So, where did this myth begin? Experiments conducted in the 1950s by the US military found that most of a person's heat was in fact lost through the head. However, the volunteers were dressed in Arctic survival suits in bitterly cold conditions, and their only exposed area was their head. Probably based on this, the *US Army Field Manual* from the 1970s claimed that 40 to 45 percent of a person's body heat is lost through the head. In situations such as this, where the body is covered and the head is exposed, a greater percentage of heat will escape from the head, and the body's core temperature will drop at a disproportionate rate. But when both the body and the head are completely covered or completely uncovered, the heat loss from the head will generally be proportional to the surface area of the head; that is, around 10 percent.

Why Can't Men See Things That Are Right in Front of Them?

Him: "Where's the butter?" Her: "In the fridge." Him: "I can't see it. It's not there." Her: "It's in the middle of the top shelf." Him: "Nope, can't see it." She then walks over and, as if by magic, grabs the butter immediately. Sound familiar? Men think this is a trick and accuse women of hiding things. Women think men deliberately play dumb purely to annoy them. Why is it that men can't seem to see things that are right in front of them?

The vision of men and women differs significantly. Women have a wider variety of cone-shaped eye cells, giving them heightened color vision, as well as wider peripheral vision. Why? Evolution.

As the women of our ancestors were nest defenders, their eyes developed to give them a broad spectrum of vision. They can see up to 45 degrees on either side of the head, as well as the same arc above and below the nose. Women evolved this way to facilitate multitasking. They were required to cook and look after the dwelling, be it a cave or otherwise, and also tend to the children and ensure their safety. They had to be alert to danger from any angle while they undertook these various tasks at the same time. Their eyes evolved this way to help them.

Men, on the other hand, were hunters, and evolved with a long-distance type of tunnel vision. This allowed them to see accurately over great distances, like a pair of binoculars. This was essential in spotting distant prey and singularly focusing on that prey while in pursuit. Peripheral vision was not as important for men, so, even now, their eyes have difficulty seeing single small objects that are nearby, especially when those objects are intermingled with other items, like the butter in the fridge.

So, ladies, don't despair. You can rest assured that the men in your life are not simply trying to annoy you. It's a biological fact that they sometimes genuinely can't see things that are right in front of them.

Why Are the Academy Awards Called the Oscars?

Every year the Academy Awards in Hollywood showcases the most talented and glamorous stars of the film industry. Since the inception of the Academy Awards in 1929, each winner is presented with a golden statuette, commonly known as an Oscar (despite its official title being the Academy Award of Merit). How did this seemingly unrelated moniker come about?

The origin of the name Oscar is disputed. The most popular theory is that the nickname was coined by the Academy librarian and future director of the Academy of Motion Picture Arts and Sciences, Margaret Herrick. It is said that when Herrick first saw the statue in 1931, she said that it looked like her Uncle Oscar, a nickname she used for her cousin Oscar Pierce. Apparently, the columnist Sidney Skolsky was there at the time and, in a 1934 *New York Daily News* article, mockingly referred to the statue as the Oscar.

Others claim that Skolsky merely took the idea from Walt Disney's Academy Award acceptance speech in 1934, when he referred to the statue as the Oscar. Skolsky continued to use the name over the ensuing years until it became the accepted name.

In the end, nobody really knows for sure how the nickname came about, but the Academy officially adopted the name Oscar for the statue in 1939, and in 2013, the Academy Awards themselves were officially rebranded as the Oscars.

❓ When People Lose Their Jobs, Why Is It Said That They Got the Sack or Got Fired?

When someone loses their job, it is commonly said that they got the sack or got fired. How did these expressions originate?

Both relate to the tools that workers used to ply their trades. When tradespeople traveled from place to place looking for work, they generally owned their tools and carried them around in a large sack. Work was often irregular, so the they never knew how long they might be employed. At the start of any given job, they would hand over their sack to their employer to look after. The employer would keep the sack for the duration of the person's employment. If the employee's services were no longer required and they were dismissed from the job, the employer would give them the sack.

To get fired originated from a time in England when miners carried their own tools from job to job. Like today, stealing was a serious offense, and any miner caught taking valuable materials, such as coal, tin, or another ore, was immediately dismissed. To prevent them from repeating their crime in another employment, their tools would also be confiscated and burned at the plant in full view of all the workers—their tools would literally get fired. Some suggest that the actual offender was set on fire in these instances, but it was likely just the tools.

To get fired was far harsher and more humiliating than to get the sack. The former was always the result of malicious behavior, while the latter was often the result of a lack of demand.

❓ Which Came First, the Chicken or the Egg?

Philosophers have always presented this dilemma as the classic unanswerable conundrum—a chicken can't exist without an egg, and vice versa—but it does have a scientific explanation. It just depends on whether the egg in question is a chicken's egg or any type of egg at all.

If the egg is any type of egg, the answer is straightforward. Over millions of years, some reptiles evolved into a birdlike dinosaur called the *Archaeopteryx*. From this animal, birdlife then evolved. The first actual bird resembling a chicken was the mutant offspring of two reptile/bird hybrids that were almost chickens, who laid an egg from which emerged the first chicken-type creature. In this case, the egg came first.

If it is assumed that the egg must be a chicken's egg, the question becomes more complex, and its answer depends on what is considered a chicken's egg. Firstly, if a hybrid chicken laid an actual chicken's egg, containing the first chicken, then the egg came first. However, if a chicken's egg is an egg that must be laid by a chicken, then a full chicken must have laid the first chicken's egg, which means that the chicken must have come first.

Combining these two ideas, a third view is that a chicken must be hatched from a chicken's egg, and that a chicken's egg must be laid by a chicken. In this case, a true chicken must have existed first in order to lay the first chicken's egg, out of which hatched a chicken. This hatched chicken would be the first chicken, despite its mother being the first true chicken.

So, while the answer depends on how the egg is defined, an answer can be reached for every scenario.

❓ What Happens If a Person Is Transfused with the Wrong Blood Type?

Everyone has one of four blood types they inherit from their parents: A, B, AB, or O. Type O is the most common, followed by A, then B, with AB the least common. All blood looks the same and we're all human, so why are the blood banks always saying they're short of a certain type of blood? What's the difference? Why can't any type of blood be used for any person?

While all blood is similar in its components—red blood cells, platelets, and plasma—it also has another important characteristic that makes it unique: antigens.

Type A blood contains proteins known as A antigens. Type B blood has B antigens, type AB blood has both A and B antigens, and type O blood has no antigens. You can't receive blood that contains an antigen different from those in your blood.

This means:

- Type O blood can be universally donated but can only be replaced by type O blood.
- Type AB blood can only be donated to people with type AB blood but can be replaced by any type of blood.
- Type A blood can only be donated to people with type A or AB blood and can only be replaced by type A or type O blood.
- Type B blood can only be donated to people with type B or AB blood and can only be replaced by type B or type O blood.

Is it a big deal if you get the wrong type of blood? Yes, a very big deal.

An ABO-incompatibility reaction can occur. If this happens, your immune system will attack the donor blood cells as if they were foreign invaders. It will produce antibodies against those foreign blood antigens and destroy them. This can lead to a variety of symptoms, including breathing difficulties, nausea, chest and abdominal pain, kidney failure, circulatory collapse, and death. Fortunately, an ABO reaction is a rare occurrence and only occurs as a result of severe human error, something that doctors are very careful to safeguard against.

How Disastrous Would the Extinction of Bees Really Be?

Bees can be an annoyance. They buzz around, land in our drinks, chase us down the street, and even sting us. For some people who are allergic, they can be a lethal threat. Yet some experts claim that if bees didn't exist, humans wouldn't exist. Albert Einstein once said that "mankind will not survive the honeybees' disappearance for more than five years." Is there any

basis to these grave allegations? Where would we be without bees?

Probably still here, but much, much hungrier.

While bees are collecting pollen, which they use as a source of protein, some of it attaches to the hairs on the bees' bodies and is inadvertently transferred to other plants, pollinating them and ensuring the next generation.

This pollination that bees perform is a vital task for the survival of agriculture. Virtually all fruits and many vegetables rely on bees for pollination, and it is estimated that bees are responsible for pollinating 80 percent of all food crops in the United States, which amounts to around $40 billion each year.

Bees literally keep plants and crops alive, and without them, crop yields would decline dramatically. This would likely have a cumulative effect up the food chain, meaning that the animals that rely on those plants for food would also be impacted, reducing the amount of meat available for people. With the supply and demand for food drastically shifting, food prices would skyrocket. Without bees, other insects may eventually take over the empty ecological niche, but in the short and medium terms, it would mean widespread economic hardship and famine, potentially posing a threat to human survival.

So, is there currently a problem? Yes. Bees are dying at an alarming rate because of pesticides, pollution, and environmental degradation. It has been estimated that in 2018 alone, up to 30 percent of the national bee population has disappeared. Experts say that this trend needs to be reversed very quickly because if the bees die out, agriculture as we know it will collapse, so there'll be a lot more to worry about than what to put on your morning toast.

❓ Why Do Only Children Get Head Lice?

Few things are more irritating, quite literally, than a bout of head lice infecting a school. Almost all the young kids are bound to get the lice, which lead to crazed stints of scratching, day and night. But have you ever noticed that while the kids in a family seem to get head lice again and again, the parents rarely do? Why is that so?

Head lice are parasitic insects that live on the scalp of people, feeding off blood and causing intense itching and irritation. The lice begin as nits, which are eggs that attach to the hair shaft. After a week, a nit hatches into a baby louse called a nymph, which matures in a week. The adult louse requires human blood to live and can survive in a person's hair for up to thirty days.

There are two main reasons why children are more susceptible to head lice than adults:

1. **Children tend to be in close contact with each other more regularly than adults.** They are generally less protective of their personal space and have more physical contact with one another. They engage in playdates, sports activities, and slumber parties. They also swap hats, use each other's hairbrushes, and share earphones. This makes it easy for head lice to travel from child to child.

2. **The pH levels of children's scalps are also a factor.** These levels are a measure of acidity. The skin of a young child has a lower level of acidity than that of an adult. When we are born, our skin pH is a neutral 7. As we grow, the body creates an acid mantle as a protective shield. This gradually increases up to the age of about twenty. This acid mantle

acts as the first barrier of defense against infections and parasites. As it's not fully developed in children, it means they are more likely to get head lice.

So, how do you stop kids from getting lice? It's a mistaken belief that lice are attracted to children who are dirty or unhygienic. The best preventative measure is for children to not share hats, clothes, or hairbrushes.

What Are the Chances We Are Alone in the Universe?

One of the most enduring questions throughout the ages has been whether us humans are alone or not. There are hundreds of billions of planets in the Milky Way and the observable universe. How likely is it that our planet is the only one that contains any form of advanced life?

Various estimates of the probability of other technologically advanced civilizations existing have been made over the years.

In 1961, University of California, Santa Cruz, astronomer and astrophysicist Frank Drake devised the Drake Equation as a way to determine whether extraterrestrial intelligent life has existed. The equation can be modified by various factors, but in simplistic terms, the chance of us being the only intelligent life in our galaxy, the Milky Way, is less than 1 in 60 billion.

In 2016, Adam Frank from the University of Rochester and Woodruff Sullivan from the University of Washington formulated a new equation based on Drake's work. By accounting for new knowledge obtained by the Kepler Space Telescope, which was launched by NASA in 2009 to survey part of the Milky Way, their calculations were more precise.

They also changed the framing of the question from "how many civilizations may exist now" to "have any ever existed." Assuming that one-fifth of all stars have habitable planets in orbit around them, they found that the odds of us being the only advanced civilization in the Milky Way are about 1 in 60 billion. Even if only one in every million stars hosts an advanced species today, that would amount to around 300,000 such civilizations in our galaxy. Frank concluded, "It is astonishingly likely that we are not the only time and place that an advanced civilization has evolved."

And that's just for our galaxy. Based on observations from the Hubble Space Telescope that NASA launched into orbit in 1990, between 125 and 250 billion galaxies are in the observable universe. Of the estimated stars that have planets orbiting them, if just one out of a billion of them has life, that would equate to approximately 6.25 billion planets. And that's just the observable universe. Who knows what's out there beyond that.

On the basis of these observations and the staggeringly large, almost incomprehensible figures, many scientists agree that it is extremely likely that other intelligent life-forms either now exist or have existed at some stage in the past.

But if that's the case, with numbers this large, why haven't we found them, or they found us?

The leading theory is that they're just too far away. Our technology is less than 200 years old, and it would take 200 years to send and receive a reply to a planet that's 100 light years away. The short life span of beings is another potential reason. Many civilizations might have already gone extinct or will evolve long after we're gone. Humans have only existed for a minute amount of time, so the chances of different civilizations overlapping in the overall scheme of time is remote.

Other potential reasons include the following: aliens lack the technology to contact us, aliens isolate themselves, Earth is deliberately not contacted, it is difficult to move great distances throughout the universe, we are not listening properly, and aliens are here undetected. Or, perhaps, the aliens are just embarrassed to be seen in their shiny silver jumpsuits.

Why Do You Have to Take Laptops Out of Their Cases at Airport Security?

Apart from removing your shoes and belt, taking your laptop out of its bag would have to be the most annoying thing a traveler is required to do. Some electronic gadgets, such as tablets and e-readers, can go through the scanner in your bag, so why does the Transportation Security Administration require your laptop to be removed and go through in its very own bin?

There are two reasons for this:

1. **To better see what's in your bag.** Most laptops and other large electronic devices, like gaming systems and DVD players, have a thick, dense battery. Because X-rays cannot usually pass through the battery, illegal items, such as a knife, could be hidden under the laptop and pass through security undetected. Removing the laptop avoids this problem.

2. **To assess the laptop itself.** Removing the laptop also allows the security personnel to get an unobstructed view of the machine itself. It may be possible to conceal certain items under the screen of a laptop, so by looking at it carefully and in isolation, it is easier to determine if this has happened.

Laptops can also be used to conceal drugs inside them. Many Colombian airport security checkpoints not only require laptops to be removed from their cases, but also turn the laptop on to ensure it is functioning properly and does not contain drugs.

The seriousness of electronic devices concealing dangerous items was brought to light in 1988 with the bombing of a Pan Am flight over Lockerbie in Scotland. In that case, a plastic explosive inside a cassette player destroyed the plane and killed 270 people.

Since the September 11 terrorist attacks, all US airports require laptops to be removed from their cases.

Do You Really Have to Wait 30 Minutes to Swim after Eating?

Many children are terrified to get into the water just after eating because it is universally accepted that swimming with a full stomach can lead to severe muscle cramping and drowning. "Wait at least thirty minutes," parents are always saying. Is it sound advice, or do parents just want a post-lunch break from supervising swimmers?

It is true that the digestive process redirects some of the blood from your muscles toward your stomach's digestive tract. This reduces the blood and oxygen levels in your limb muscles, and may reduce their efficient functioning. This could potentially cause cramping, but it's unlikely. Cramps are involuntary, spasmodic contractions of the muscles, usually caused by a variety of factors, predominantly dehydration. The mere fact that your digestive system is working would not usually starve the other muscles of so much blood that they would cramp.

Another suggested reason for not swimming after eating is the potential for getting a stitch. A stitch is a sharp, stabbing pain, usually under the rib cage. While it's not entirely clear what causes a stitch, it's likely related to dehydration or a redirection of blood away from the diaphragm during exercise. A stitch typically results from exercise, which includes swimming, but it is not of serious concern, and the fact that you've eaten beforehand may not increase your chances of getting a stitch.

While there is a theoretical possibility that someone could get a cramp or a stitch while swimming just after eating, it is extremely unlikely that a person would then drown as a result. A swimmer could easily exit the water if this occurred or make their way to shallower waters and simply stand up.

There are no official guidelines or warnings in relation to swimming after eating. Indeed, an incident of drowning from swimming on a full stomach has never been documented, and there's no research to confirm the popular belief.

Why Do People Get Dizzy If Spun Around?

When a person spins repeatedly in circles, a sensation of dizziness or vertigo will often result. This happens because the hairlike sensory nerve cells in the inner ear send incorrect signals to the brain.

The body senses its position and its motion through the vestibular system, which is contained in the upper part of the inner ear and consists of canals that contain the hairlike sensory nerve cells as well as a fluid called endolymph, which, because of inertia, resists any change in motion. When we spin around, the endolymph lags behind and stimulates the hairlike cells to signal to the brain that the head is spinning. When the endolymph starts to move at the same rate as that at which we're spinning, it no longer stimulates the hairlike cells and the brain adapts to the motion. When the spinning stops, however, the endolymph keeps moving, and this motion again stimulates the hairlike cells, which fire signals to the brain, which in turn interprets these erroneous messages as signifying that spinning is still occurring, causing dizziness. Once the endolymph stops moving, the signals stop, and the brain realizes that the spinning has ceased. The dizziness then subsides.

After spinning around in one direction, if a person then reverses directions, the dizziness isn't as acute, because the change in direction helps to stop the endolymph from moving, and the two directions of spinning cancel each other out.

If You Touch a Baby Bird, Will Its Mother Really Reject It?

Most people know that you should never touch a baby bird or a bird's egg. If you do, the mother bird will reject the bird immediately before abandoning the nest. The theory is that wild birds are so sensitive to the dangers posed by humans that they will fly away if they catch even the faintest whiff of human scent on their young. Is this true?

No, not at all. Despite how timid birds may be, they do not readily abandon their young, and certainly not in response to human touch. The myth probably comes from the belief that birds can detect the faintest human smell, but this is not true. Birds actually have relatively small and simple olfactory nerves, which limits their sense of smell. There are exceptions to this, such as the vulture, who has evolved to have a good sense of smell, but most birds cannot smell well and would be very unlikely to discern the scent of a human.

Even if a bird were able to detect your scent and make a negative association with it, it is still unlikely to reject its chicks. Like most animals, birds have an innate drive to nurture their offspring, are usually very devoted to them, and are not easily deterred from taking care of them. This is particularly so as the chicks get older, because the bird will have invested more time into the babies and will not want to see its efforts go to waste.

That said, if you do see a baby bird on the ground, as a general rule, leave it alone. It is normal for a fledgling bird to spend a few days on the ground while it's mastering its flying skills, and the bird's parents will likely be watching its progression from a distance. It is only if a bird is in a very unsafe area, such as on a road or in the vicinity of some prowling cats, that you should gently pick up the chick and put it back into its nest. And, if you do this, fear not; the bird's parents will welcome it back with open wings.

What Makes Grumpy Old Men Grumpy?

We've all seen him many times, with the scowling face, the shaking head, the aggressive tone—the grumpy old man. What is he grumpy about? Anything and everything: the government, the economy, the state of the sidewalk, teenagers, the chirping birds. But why? Were Jack Lemmon and Walter Matthau acting in *Grumpy Old Men*, or is that just how they are?

Also known as *grumpy old man complex* or *irritable male syndrome*, the crankiness of many older gentlemen can be attributed to a number of factors.

Psychology plays a major role. By the age of sixty or seventy, many men have retired from work or are approaching retirement. A feeling of worthlessness can result, like that of being thrown on the scrap heap, with daunting thoughts of a future sitting around the home with no aspirations left to attain. As friends and loved ones die, men can become aware of their own mortality and health problems, resulting in depression and anxiety. Men tend to suppress these concerns, leaving them prone to anger and outbursts directed toward other people or situations, for whatever trivial reason.

In addition to emotional changes, changes in an old man's brain are the main root of the condition. As men age, testosterone levels fall, usually significantly by age sixty. By seventy, they tend to be at half the level of a young man, indicating a kind of male menopause. A decrease in testosterone typically leads to fatigue, depression, and a reduction in libido and powers of concentration. This often leads to irritability and an inability to deal with the nuances of everyday life. The result? A grumpy old man.

But it's not just men. Irritable male syndrome has been noticed in the animal kingdom with red deer, reindeer, sheep, and Indian elephants. During breeding, when testosterone levels are high, these males are confident and competent. However, as the mating season ends and their testosterone drops, they become nervous and agitated, often striking out irrationally.

In addition to a drop in testosterone in older men, another key change takes place. They lose brain tissue in the frontal lobe region at almost three times the rate of women. The frontal lobes are involved in motor function, memory, problem-solving, concentration, reasoning, and impulse control.

So, the next time an old man goes berserk at you for stepping foot on his lawn, remember that he's not pretending to be Clint Eastwood out of *Gran Torino*. There's a physiological reason for his behavior, and it's not all his fault. Try to wave, smile, and blame biology.

Why Do Wounds Itch as They're Healing?

As any wound on the skin starts to heal, it itches. Why?

There are two reasons.

1. The skin contains nerve fibers that detect when the dermis (one of the upper layers of the skin) is being irritated. Those fibers then send a signal to the brain telling it that there is an itch. This is known as a mechanical stress, which is done to warn the brain about a potential danger.

When a wound heals, the cells around the wound increase at its base, joining together and contracting to pull the wound shut. This produces a mechanical stress similar to an irritation. The nerve fibers alert the brain, which results in an itch.

2. The body releases a chemical called histamine in response to a wound in an attempt to prevent bacteria from entering the wound. The histamine is released at the site of the wound, and because it is not normally found there, its presence stimulates the nerve fibers, which cause us to itch.

An itchy healing wound is a positive sign, meaning that our systems are functioning correctly. It's just bad luck if the healing wound happens to be in the middle of your back, or worse still, under a plaster cast.

Is It Dangerous to Be in a Swimming Pool during a Thunderstorm?

If you're swimming in a pool and a thunderstorm starts building, the first thing you'll see is people getting out of the water, and the first thing you'll hear, apart from the thunder, is the panic-stricken warnings from people to get out of the water immediately. Should these warnings be heeded, or are you okay to swim on?

Heed the warnings.

Lightning is random and unpredictable. An electrical discharge seeks the shortest path to the ground, which is not only measured in distance, but also in resistivity. This means lightning will often hit the most conductive thing around. Since water is an excellent conductor of electricity, this is often a body of water.

For a number of reasons, it's dangerous to be in a swimming pool if lightning is around. Because the water is a good conductor, it will attract the lightning. But for you to be in danger, the lightning doesn't actually have to strike you directly. If it strikes the water near to you, the current may still give you a fatal shock. Swimming pools are also connected to a much larger surface area via underground water pipes and electric wiring for filters and lights. If the lightning strikes the ground anywhere along this conductive network, it could produce a shock in the pool itself.

It is not uncommon for swimmers to get struck by lightning and there are a number of examples, including three people getting struck in the ocean near Tampa in 2005. Fish in open waters also get killed, but as most of the lightning current flows across the surface of the water, many fish that swim deeper remain unaffected.

The National Lightning Safety Institute recommends a very conservative approach toward swimming during a thunderstorm. Any time you hear thunder, you should immediately get out of the water and into a safe place. And all pool activities should be suspended until at least thirty minutes after the last clap of thunder is heard. The upshot: swimming during a thunderstorm is one of the most dangerous things you can do.

Why Does Coffee Make You Poop?

Picture the scene: In a rush for work, you take a shower and get dressed, then have a quick cup of coffee before you run out the door. You jump in the car and are about to set off when they strike—the coffee poops. Just what is it about that life-saving cup of coffee that makes you need the toilet?

While it is thought that about one-third of coffee drinkers experience this reaction, it is still unknown exactly what causes it.

Caffeine was generally believed to be the culprit, its stimulating effect activating contractions in the colon and intestinal muscles. However, while caffeinated coffee does tend to result in more people experiencing the coffee poops, decaf can also have the same effect, indicating that there are other ingredients in coffee that may also be responsible.

It is known that both forms of coffee stimulate the digestive hormones gastrin and cholecystokinin, which promote a response called the gastrocolic reflex, resulting in stomach contractions that increase the urge to poop. It is still not clear how coffee stimulates these hormones, but it may be that the simple act of drinking a liquid increases the reaction, especially in the morning when the body's digestive system kicks into gear.

Coffee also contains chlorogenic acid, and there is another theory that the acidity levels of coffee result in an increased production of gastric acid in the stomach that stimulates the bowels.

Adding milk or cream may also promote the coffee poops, especially if the consumer has a lactose intolerance, as may the addition of sugar or sugar substitutes.

It is also thought that the beans and oils in coffee may also be a factor, although the reasons are again unclear.

So, while scientists have not pinpointed the exact reason why coffee makes you poop, there are likely to be a variety of factors involved, and whether you drink regular coffee or decaf, there's a good chance you'll be affected—and that's the bottom line.

ARTWORK CREDITS

About the Author

Andrew Thompson divides his time between Australia and England. A lawyer by trade, his obsession with finding out the truth about aspects of the world that we take for granted has led him to accumulate a vast body of knowledge, which he has distilled into book form. He is the author of five Ulysses Press bestsellers: *What Did We Use Before Toilet Paper?*, *Can Holding in a Fart Kill You?*, *Hair of the Dog to Paint the Town Red*, *Why Do Roller Coasters Make You Puke?*, and *Back In The Day*. See all of Andrew's books at www.andrewthompsonwriter.co.uk or on Twitter @AndrewTWriter.